# Disorganized Crime

## Defendants, Inmates, and Victims with Disabilities

# Disorganized Crime

## Defendants, Inmates, and Victims with Disabilities

Nancy Cowardin, Ph.D.

Thunderbird PRESS

The purpose of this book is to educate the criminal justice system, adjunct professionals, and the general public so they may better identify and accommodate cognitive disabilities. Fictitious names have been used throughout the book in order to protect the anonymity of all disabled defendants, inmates, and victims. For this same reason, case locations and dates of occurrence were omitted in some instances. The author referenced actual case materials to insure accuracy wherever possible. Where case files were incomplete or otherwise destroyed, details related to the timing and order of events were supplied to the best of her recollection.

Thunderbird Press, P.O. Box 524, Rancho Mirage, CA 92270, thunderbirdpress@dc.rr.com

Book design by Jean Denning
Cover art by Nancy Cowardin, Ph.D.
Cover design by Karoline Kessler

Library of Congress Control Number: 2019917325

Cowardin, Nancy
*Disorganized Crime*
*Defendants, Inmates, and Victims with Disabilities*
ISBN: 978-0-578-59832-1

Printed in the United States of America

*For Dave, who understands,*

*and Devin, who needs to know.*

# ACKNOWLEDGMENTS

I am indebted to the many wonderful friends who supported me throughout this project, with special thanks to three women from my book club who agreed to read and edit sample chapters in their early stages: Elizabeth, for her "great catch" in Chapter Four; Helen, for her brilliant and insightful comments and suggestions; and Bonnie, with Leonard by her side, for her continual friendship and encouragement. Thanks also to Ernie Galvan for his wisdom and Marie and Sal DiVita for generously pointing me in the right direction.

Enormous thanks are lovingly extended to my cheerleader and confidant, Dave Cowardin. No husband could have been more supportive throughout all stages of this project.

I wish to acknowledge and express my admiration to the numerous criminal justice professionals who took on the difficult task of accommodating disabilities in our shared clients. In order to protect the anonymity of all concerned, most of you remain unnamed in this book. Nevertheless, you know who you are and should feel a great deal of pride in your extraordinary efforts. In those instances where attorneys, judges, sentencing advocates, and law enforcement officers worked together toward compassionate understanding, fundamental fairness did indeed prevail.

Let me make it clear that it is *never* the intention of disability advocates to excuse criminal behavior nor to ignore the suffering of victims. On the contrary, each team of professionals tasked with handling a case involving cognitive disabilities sought to present as complete a picture of the defendant as possible in order to assist the Court in matching the punishment to both the crime AND the perpetrator. A big thank you to the judges who asked the right questions and the jurors who listened with open minds. Thank you, also, to the many victims' families who opted for more merciful penalties once they understood the limited competence and capacity of the hapless defendants before them.

Last, I would like to express thanks to my editor, Jean Denning, at Thunderbird Press, for her sharp eye and patient guidance. Working her magic, Jean whipped a slew of preliminary chapters into the professional presentation that eventually took shape. Thanks, also, to Jean's graphic designer and InDesign specialist, Karoline Kessler, for her completed cover design and for converting the manuscript to InDesign.

# PREFACE

Fifteen-year-old Omar had just begun his sophomore year at a new high school, fresh from a self-contained special education class in his previous district. Unfortunately, as is sometimes the case, his files didn't show up in time to place Omar in a setting where he could get the help he, as a non-reader with a team-diagnosed Learning Disability, desperately needed. Instead, the boy was enrolled in a standard English II class with a teacher whose negligent ignorance about his disability, along with her petulant and vengeful attitude in the situation that followed, fueled and prompted the whole sorry incident.

I agreed to take Omar as my first forensic client because what happened seemed to me a sadly predictable calamity that could have been prevented if all concerned had just listened to the boy and done their jobs. I was, at the time, serving as the Director of Community Outreach at a private center that catered to individuals with special needs. It was there, while writing and administering early intervention and juvenile justice grants, that I was asked to evaluate this tenth grader by a juvenile division Public Defender who sat on our Board of Directors. She was convinced that Omar had no intention of actually killing his teacher, but had merely reacted impulsively after being shamed in front of his classmates. This happened in 1989, well before anyone thought of installing metal detectors in the gates of public high schools. In fact, Omar's knife assault may have been the final straw that led to this now common practice.

On the day in question, Omar was assigned an in-class task that he feared would amplify his academic problems in front of the new peer group. So, the youth did what many others have done before him—he acted out in hopes of a) gaining peer esteem as a tough guy, and/or b) being ejected from the classroom to avoid the embarrassing task altogether. I might add that Omar had visited his counselor twice in the past two months to initiate a special education transfer but was roundly ignored. Now put on the spot by a request to read something aloud, the youth became sullen and noncompliant, an attitude that never fails to provoke a teacher's wrath. After some back and forth, she put the boy's name on the blackboard for after-school discipline. Omar went up and erased it. When she returned to the board and put his name up *a second time*, the mounting cheers and jeers of the class pushed the boy over the edge. He again erased the board and turned to walk back to his seat. At this time, the teacher sat at her desk facing the class with her back to the blackboard. This was when Omar, trying to act casual in the fracas, reached both hands into his pockets and discovered a small pen knife in one of them. There sat the teacher spouting on about additional penalties, her unprotected shoulder protruding slightly into the aisle, so Omar opened his penknife and stabbed a one-inch gash in it. Criminal charge: Attempted murder.

✧ ✧ ✧

Now, it is not my intention to portray this boy as a completely innocent victim, but rather to illustrate how a) our public schools and this particular teacher fueled Omar's frustration by failing to address his particular needs and, subsequently, b) the behavior that ensued did not arise "out of the blue." Indeed, this is a case where A yields B. That's because observant, committed caregivers—and this includes teachers—can detect and head off problems well before they erupt into catastrophes. Had the sending school district forwarded Omar's records, correct placement would have occurred. Had the new guidance counselor actually listened to the student and followed up with a phone call, similar assistance might have been obtained. Had his teacher bothered to assess and accommodate Omar's skill deficits, she could have provided more suitable classroom tasks. And finally, had this teacher understood that backing a teenager up against a wall in front of his peers amounts to a dangerous game of "chicken," she could have handled things differently. Instead we see an entirely preventable disaster that affected everyone involved, cost the taxpayers money, and greatly impacted a kid's future life. That was my first case three decades ago, and I still wonder how Omar fared later in adulthood. Oh sure, his attorney managed to get a reduced sentence handled entirely within the juvenile system, but the kid would be branded as a troublemaker indefinitely.

Once word about Omar's semi-successful case outcome hit the public defender pipeline, my phone started ringing off the hook. It seems I had suddenly acquired a new professional identity as a "forensic expert" that was quite unintentional. Within two weeks I was assigned my first death penalty case. That fascinating case ("John") is fully addressed in Chapter Five. Suffice to say that the local defense community was hungry for information about any links between learning disabilities and criminal behavior. Rather quickly, I found myself appointed on dozens of new cases—some juvenile, but mostly adult—and was invited to speak at several state and federal defense-related conferences. These appearances, in turn, resulted in hundreds more case appointments, trainings, and lectures throughout the state of California, as well as in twenty-one other states and the District of Columbia.

The chapters that follow describe a number of memorable cases in which I was appointed to assess and fully delineate the cognitive disabilities either documented or suggested in existing file materials. To do this, I traveled to each assigned housing location armed with court orders that would enable me access to the clients in private, face-to-face settings. These documents typically requested that the inmate's hands be free of restraints so he could write on test protocols, utilize a hand-held computer microswitch, and handle any other manipulative materials that might be required for the assessment. I tried to connect with these individuals on a basic human level, taking time to explain my role, obtain a simple life history, gauge their current wellbeing, and answer any questions I could about their pending cases. I usually requested that a lunch tray be brought to them inside the testing room and that escorted bathroom breaks be provided as needed. Closely monitoring these individuals for fatigue and any frustration behaviors that might surface, I was able to make the rather lengthy test session move along quite successfully and at a good pace. More importantly, I chose materials that made testing interactive, informative, and even somewhat fun. Due to these uniform precautions, fewer than ten inmates out of the more than eight hundred whom I tested became overwrought or otherwise uncooperative enough to abort the process.

Now in retirement, I often smile in thinking back to the twenty-five years I served as a forensic assessor and expert. This was the finest work of my life which resulted in meaningful and long-lasting positive change, not only for individual clients with cognitive disabilities, but in a host of subsequent class action lawsuits against the California prison and parole systems where similar plaintiffs alleged personal violations under the 1990 Americans with Disabilities Act. I've traveled a lot of ground since I entered that first juvenile hall to test Omar, literally shaking in my boots as the gates clanged shut behind me. Things only worsened when I visited Los Angeles' Men's Central Jail facility for the first time two weeks later and had to pass through *two* such locked barriers to the outside world in order to interview John inside the attorney room. How quickly these initially fearful experiences became part of my necessary routine to discover and explain cognitive disabilities in defendants, inmates, and parolees. After ten years of trying to balance my work at the private center with a burgeoning caseload of these criminal clients, I quit the former job in order to devote full time to issues of *fundamental fairness* in the criminal justice process. These case studies document some of the most memorable and rewarding experiences in that career.

In the end, the primary objective of this book, and my job as a disability advocate, was and is to educate those who will come in contact with similar defendants, inmates, and victims in the future. In all "mainstreaming" and "normalization" efforts, Step One is always *awareness*—knowledge that the person with a disability exists and now requires accommodation. Hopefully, this book goes some of the distance toward achieving that goal. Step Two involves so-called *service interactions* in both business and casual contexts that will maximize meaningful participation by a disabled individual. The vast array of behaviors that facilitate such interactions cannot be learned by simply reading a book, but must be gained through collaborative experience on a case-by-case basis. I therefore urge members of the helping professions (psychology, education, social work) to enlarge their spheres of expertise, join with criminal justice professionals, and take up the challenge. *Fundamental fairness* is worth fighting for.

# GROUND RULES

Tom wasn't what I had expected—not Latino, not black, not a gang banger—just a nice looking white kid from the Los Angeles suburbs. I had been asked by his defense attorney to visit and assess the twenty-year-old at a Central Valley prison as part of an appeal of his life sentence for a drug purchase gone wrong. The drug dealer's subsequent death resulted in all five of the would-be buyers receiving life sentences from a judge facing public condemnation for having meted out light sentences in two celebrity drug possession cases. Publicity about the case touched a nerve on the national level, prompting a lengthy article in a major "pop culture" magazine. Now sitting across a desk from Tom, I realized that his attorney had simply been "fishing" in hopes that I might discover some sort of learning disability as mitigating evidence. Instead, I found a sharp, conversational, fairly well-educated young man from a "good home." Charmed by his engaging manner, I momentarily lost focus and heard myself asking, "How the heck did you end up here?" His chillingly accurate response has stayed with me these many years and should serve as a warning to *all* parents: *"It only takes a second."*

I knew only too well what he meant: one second of confusion that leads to a bad decision; one second when someone flips you a knife in a fight; one second of intense fear or provoked anger—especially when combined with the reduced competence that characterizes my "usual" cognitively disabled clients. Tom wasn't one of them.

This interesting, though futile, experience prompted a "note to self" that became **Ground Rule #1** in my practice: Always inquire up front as to why a referring attorney thinks my expertise would benefit his or her case. What did he or she discover in the client's file, or via family member interviews, that suggested a cognitive disorder was present? How did he or she expect my findings and report to help mitigate the guilt and/or penalty phases of the case? How serious and/or realistic was the attorney in this regard?

I'm reminded of an email I once received from an out-of-state mitigation specialist entitled, "Can you make our client retarded?"

My answer: "No, he'd have to do that on his own."

I've sat in jails and prisons throughout the country assessing defendants, inmates, and parolees of all ages in quiet testing rooms, glass cubicles, hastily-arranged medical exam rooms, and even padded cells. And since it takes several hours, or even days, to conduct a thorough assessment, I usually became fairly familiar with the workings of the facilities themselves. In the ever-expanding network of America's barred facilities, some were more memorable than others for being efficient and compassionate (e.g., Sacramento's downtown jail); or, conversely, as punitive and as user-*unfriendly* as they could possibly be (e.g., the infamous Riker's Island complex). Generally speaking, the one common thread running through these institutions was to facilitate administrative convenience and benefit. In other words, policies were put in place to streamline and simplify daily routine, keep law suits at bay, and minimize discomfort for the staff, *not* the inmates nor the public. Permit me to share a memory here that will illustrate my point.

Over the period of one week, I conducted two assessments inside the same county jail medical unit. Week one, I tested a 6'8" defendant charged with three rapes, the last of which resulted in a murder, thereby making it a capital case. Week two, I saw a middle-aged man, shorter than myself, who was accused of child endangerment in a case which had, unfortunately, become newsworthy. You see, even though he had moderate intellectual impairments which affected judgment, Defendant #2 had been left to watch his estranged wife's home daycare business while she went shopping. When a toddler became muddy playing in the yard, the defendant filled the bath tub with hot (only) water, adding lots of caustic bubble bath, stripped the little girl, and put her in to soak. He had no knowledge that the water heater had been turned up to 127 degrees, nor did he check the bath temperature manually. In the moments it took for the child to begin crying and the defendant to stop ignoring her and react appropriately, serious widespread burns occurred. Ineffective first aid (rubbing butter on the child's legs and buttocks) only made matters worse. The county now faced a gigantic lawsuit for licensing such inadequate care and the defendant was criminally charged.

In contrast, my 6'8" week #1 client suffered from such severe emotional liability (unpredictable and/or cyclic ups and downs) that I had to arrange three separate visits in two holding locations to complete his assessment. This was our final meeting. Because the testing rooms were mostly occupied that day, the deputy on duty unlocked a small office off the main patrolled hallway and ushered us inside. The space in this tiny unventilated room was entirely filled by one small desk and two chairs. I quickly became uncomfortable because, sitting behind the desk, I faced the exit door with its 8x10" window looking out on an empty hallway. Meanwhile, the defendant sat opposite me, blocking the door with his enormous body. Not good, especially when you consider that all three of his crimes were against women, and that he seemed extremely moody and depressed that particular day. Luckily, I was able to cut the assessment rather short, having already amassed a good deal of usable data in our two previous visits.

Now, let's return to week #2, where my small, pathetic, and quite harmless client was placed in the largest testing room in the unit, directly across from a monitored control booth, AND I was informed that a deputy must sit in the room throughout the assessment. I objected to this highly unusual stipulation due to the confidential nature of test content, not to mention the privacy rights of any test taker; but I was assured that this was a court-ordered necessity due to the high profile status of his current case. I repeated my objection, pointing out that I was left alone with a powerful rape-murderer just last week. What did they think this little guy was going to do—*give me a bath?* But, you see, that was when it finally dawned on me: this was never about my safety or the seriousness of the crime; it was merely "CYA" and administrative convenience.

So, there you have the unfortunate truth, as well as my personal **Ground Rule #2:** Never assume that jail staff are there for either support or protection. They have a job to do. I was lucky if they unlocked the testing room door to afford me bathroom breaks. They won't run after anyone who inadvertently leaves anything behind. Trust me, I know this because I left my purse in the testing room my first time in Men's Central Jail, Los Angeles. The young deputy's sarcastic response when I hastily returned there: "This isn't a good place to leave your purse, Ma'am." I never brought a purse inside again. In some cases, visitors are even required to sign an agreement acknowledging that staff will not intervene on your behalf should a hostage situation occur. Do they really mean this? I don't know and was careful to never find out.

Over the years, I also saw how jails and prisons dealt with the human aspect of the guard-versus-prisoner relationship. For example, I spent more than enough time testing six condemned men inside Oklahoma's McAlester Prison to learn that inmates from the Unit A take that final walk to the death chamber escorted by Unit B guards and vice versa. Why? Because this reciprocal policy lifts a sad burden off the shoulders of prison guards who have become friendly with inmates assigned to their own units via casual interactions, shooting baskets in the interior court, or late night card games.

This leads me to **Ground Rule #3:** Correctional staff may effect a humorless and authoritarian facade, but they are also human beings with real feelings. I soon learned to treat them accordingly, both because they deserved it as people serving a unique capacity, and because they could make my visit very unpleasant if I didn't. In this regard, I have gone to the trouble of bringing special treats (e.g., cookies, Starbucks coffee) to particularly helpful staff members and even drove several large yard decorations to a retiring deputy in the Sacramento Jail. I've never been sorry for acknowledging our shared humanity, and believe that doing so extends more of the same into their future interactions.

My multiple appointments at Oklahoma's McAlester ("Big Mac") Prison were in response to the Supreme Court's verdict in the 2002 *Atkins* case (*Atkins v. Virginia, 536 U.S. 304*) which vacated the death penalty in favor of a life sentence for inmates with severe intellectual impairments. The thinking behind this decision, correct in my opinion, was that adults with childlike minds cannot be held fully responsible for their actions no matter how heinous the typically unintended outcome. Often described as "guilty but not responsible," these individuals, like my week #2 client at the Los Angeles jail, deserve punishment—but in a manner better suited to their capacity to form intent, their competence as self-advocates in the trial process, and their ability to effect meaningful behavioral change as a result.

"Don't let them bury me here," begged Ben, one of the McAlester inmates who had not qualified with any type of formal intellectual impairment despite the hopes of his defense team. He, like the others under post-Atkins appeal, had seen the prison's on-grounds cemetery and balked at being laid to rest under a flat stone engraved with only his inmate ID number. Now, a jar containing Ben's ashes rests on a shelf in his appeal attorney's office, flanked by several others who didn't meet the Supreme Court standard.

Did I beat myself up for not "saving" Ben by alleging disabilities that weren't present? My "no" answer to this question has everything to do with **Ground Rule #4:** Always report fully and honestly, both on paper and in oral testimony. Why? Because fudging any data or diagnoses could lead to several undesirable outcomes, both personally and professionally. First among these would be the devastating effect such behavior would have on my personal integrity and my reputation as a "straight shooter." Once word of my indiscretions became known, prosecutors would have a field day with me on cross examination, and I would be drummed out of the business. But most importantly, a loss of credibility would limit my use in future cases where actual disabilities were present and required explanation as mitigating factors. Indeed, losing future opportunities to insure the *fundamental fairness* that was central to my work as a disability advocate would be the heaviest price to pay.

Several rather logistical notes to self comprise **Ground Rule #5:** Learn the rules of each particular housing location before making the trek to the facility. Some prisons prohibit clothing in so-called "gang colors," while others shun denim or certain quirky color combinations for no apparent reason. I once showed up at a central valley prison wearing a gold-colored suit with a brown silk blouse, only to be told brown pants with yellow shirts were prohibited. Fortunately, since my colors were reversed top to bottom (and it was an all-male prison to boot), they let me in. Black became my safest option. Many others prohibit sleeveless blouses and open necklines. A strangely unrealistic concern that underwires can easily be removed from bras and weaponized has led to their prohibition at some locations but not others. As a result, my standard jail uniform now includes a sports bra. Would it be okay to bring my lunch in? How about insulin or other prescription medications? If it's raining, would they prohibit a small folding umbrella? What are bad times to enter or exit due to staff shift changes? Better to be prepared than forced to go braless, wait an extra hour for the shift change to conclude, or be denied admission altogether.

And finally, **Ground Rule #6:** This "rule" is intended to assist the reader in clearing up any confusion about past and current disability terminology. Please remember in reading these chapters that the vast majority of file data, referral and court documents, and even my own forensic reports originated some ten to twenty or more years ago. Back then, terms for the various disabilities were different and have been overhauled to be more "politically correct" in the years since. So, when I quote charges, school documents, or other sources using now archaic terms, please understand that it is not my intention to malign or denigrate anyone. I have included updated terms where possible, but a few of the old ones will undoubtedly slip through. Both *Appendix A* and the *Glossary* to this book provide guidelines that will help clarify and update labels and other terms of the trade used in the book. Nevertheless, much of this terminology is still in flux; thus, what's in vogue today may become outdated tomorrow.

When I speak at legal conferences or write explanatory articles, I try to use titles that reflect the cognitive states of past clients who suffered from a formal Learning Disability (LD); an Intellectual Disability (ID), which, as noted above, replaced the demeaning term, mental retardation; and/or an Attention Deficit Disorder (ADD).

Titles like Unintended Consequences, Hidden Disabilities, and Crimes of Innocence aptly describe *some* of these individuals and the actions that led to their current situations, while others are less easily pegged. Because the discussions that follow cover all three disability categories, choosing one all-inclusive title became challenging. Nevertheless, Disorganized Crime won out because it is precisely this sort of *cognitive disorganization* that best characterizes how people with LD, ID, and ADD think and behave when they are under stress. Indeed, Tom's insightful remark that it "only takes a second" is even more fitting in cases where the impulsive, bungled, immature reactions associated with these cognitive disorders come into play.

# CONTENTS



Continued ...

Continued ...

# PART ONE

# Learning, Attention, and Language Disabilities

# CHAPTER ONE
## J.R., Eight Years on Death Row

I sat in the hallway just outside Angola Prison's Death Row unit awaiting admission. Arranging a suitable, private space for the sort of psychoeducational assessment which I was court-ordered to conduct can take some time, so I used it to organize and prepare some of J.R.'s test protocols in advance. With that task completed, I began perusing the various notifications and signs in the hallway where my attention landed on a grid of small photos posted inside a glass case. I walked over to get a better look and realized that these one hundred or so men were, indeed, the residents of Angola's Death Row. Although the head-shot photos resembled those taken yearly in grammar schools nationwide, the array comprising this rather macabre Hall of Fame served a very different purpose; namely, easy visual identification should an emergency situation occur. It didn't take more than a few seconds for me to absorb the fact that no more than five of these inmates were Caucasian. *Welcome to the South*, I thought.

In fact, welcome to being poor, black, and disabled in Louisiana, with the additional benefit of having an overworked Public Defender as your only advocate before an all-white jury. Add to that the public outrage surrounding black-on-white crime, in this case, a killing in broad daylight on a busy Baton Rouge street. That scenario pretty well summed up J.R.'s original trial eight years prior, but now his luck had changed: his habeas case had been picked up, pro bono, by the appeals division of a high-powered law firm. How Marie, a local sentencing advocate, had managed this pairing I still don't know; but sure enough, a law firm situated on the top floor of New Orleans' tallest building was now involved. Getting to know this amazing woman better in the months that followed, I quickly realized that, despite her relaxed southern manner and Buddhist grounding, her dedication to truth and justice was fiercely unrelenting. She was also the reason that I became involved in what was to be the single most rewarding case of my career as a forensic assessor.

## J.R.'s Background

I had just stepped away from the podium at a national legal defense conference in Chicago when Marie approached me. She offered to accompany me to lunch and, now practically starving, I accepted. Over our salads, she laid out J.R.'s history and the habeas (appeal) efforts in his capital case thus far. It was quite a story. The now twenty-six-year-old inmate was born to a deaf single mother whose oral and written language was virtually nonexistent. His father could have been any one of several brief acquaintances and most likely remained totally unaware of the boy's existence. There was some speculation that J.R. may have been an "occupational hazard" on his mother's part, but this was never confirmed. Whatever the case, lacking financial and social support, mother and son remained fairly isolated within the sizeable city of Baton Rouge, where communication was accomplished through standard gestures interspersed with a slang form of American Sign Language (ASL).

Kids with mothers like J.R.'s generally learn early to communicate via gesture rather than speech. I'm reminded of a pair of brothers at a Head Start we serviced in East Los Angeles whose mother, though hearing, remained essentially non-lingual in most daily interactions. This was partially due to a family taboo against talking to babies, pets, or anyone else who could not respond. In fact, this mother had initially talked to the older brother as a baby, but stopped when a relative threatened to have her committed as a lunatic if such stupid and meaningless conversation continued. As a result, both preschool boys demonstrated severe language delays, relying largely on grunts and gestures, and required direct intervention to prepare them for kindergarten. Mom also needed our help—first to support her in abandoning her family taboo and standing up to meddling relatives, and second to relearn how to communicate with her young children. Our efforts in this case were highly successful because the boys' mother could hear and was willing to learn. However, in J.R.'s case, no such intervention was attempted, nor would one have been effective for a parent whose lifelong disability precluded the development of oral language.

Due to the isolated symbiotic existence of this mother and son team, preschool was never sought as a corrective option. Likewise, kindergarten was skipped altogether because J.R.'s illiterate parent remained unaware of class availability and locations. Accordingly, when the boy enrolled in first grade, teachers immediately observed him to be sorely backward in both language and school readiness. This led to his first referral for special education services in the form of weekly speech and language therapy.

In a telephone interview, J.R.'s earliest speech therapist recalled that it took a period of two full years to correct the boy's articulation problems. Meanwhile, his *processing* (composition and understanding) of oral language, both expressively and receptively, comprised an additional remedial struggle that lasted a total of four years. One notation in the therapist's file showed that, at just over eight and one-half years of age, J.R.'s ability to receive and process oral language scored at the four-year level on a standardized test, coding a "severe" age deficit. In fact, if one computes a "Verbal IQ" using these data, the youngster would have scored in the low 50s for his age band. This extreme reduction demonstrates the developmental impact of J.R.'s isolated existence with a nonlingual mother, paired with very limited out-of-home experiences involving language interactions.

By the time J.R. had advanced to the fourth grade, widening academic lags in all subjects formally qualified him as having a Specific Learning Disability (SLD) under Louisiana's state codes. The fact that the boy was already receiving speech and language therapy meant simply extending special education services to address his now critical academic deficits. This was accomplished by placing him in a pull-out program which afforded partial day remedial help. Over the next few years, a school-based placement team repeatedly documented J.R.'s academic discrepancies and prescribed regular interventions, but little advancement followed. Instead, he reached a sort of skills plateau that hovered just at, and later dipped below, the commonly accepted "literacy level" needed for the most minimal adult competence. No advancement occurred past this point, and the discouraged youth dropped out of school at the age of seventeen.

Just for a second, imagine how you might react if your own seventeen-year-old one day simply *stopped* going to school. Even if you didn't immediately notice his new laid-back lifestyle, it wouldn't be long before the school attendance office was threatening to send a truancy officer to your home. Contact would initially be made via several phone calls, with follow-up notification on district letterhead if the minor's attendance didn't improve. You would then be hauled into the district office and made to account for your failure, as a parent, to facilitate your son's daily attendance. If warnings didn't work, you might be sent to a local review board (known as SARB: School Action Review Board, in California) with potentially disastrous consequences if you failed to improve your son's subsequent attendance. I have seen similar situations where a family's welfare checks were threatened, fines were imposed, and even criminal charges were tossed around.

So, knowing how seriously truancy is treated elsewhere, I again marvel at how J.R. simply walked away from school. Of course, his mother's social isolation and undeveloped reading skills had to be major factors here, exacerbated by the school district's inability to find and employ an appropriate intermediary interpreter. Almost certainly J.R.'s generalized failure to advance academically and, at seventeen, being close to "aging out" anyway, probably accounted for the district's nonexistent efforts to reel him back into the fray. In any case, all of these factors resulted in the inept drop-out whose inborn learning disabilities got the better of him in the end. So, let's tackle this head on: What, exactly, is a Specific Learning Disability anyway?

## Specific Learning Disability

The degree to which having any sort of learning disability affects a child's self concept depends very much on other supportive factors in his or her life. For example, a loving, involved family with the financial wherewithal to provide a wealth of experiences goes a long way toward both adapting to deficits and easing the pain of being "different." Caring parents will go to great lengths to identify other areas in which their learning disabled child excels (e.g., sports, art, music) and to make these equally important to academic achievement in the home. Conversely, such disabilities can present insurmountable hurdles for children from a home situation like J.R.'s, where maternal deafness and associated isolation, poverty, illiteracy, and ongoing family stress create firm barriers to success.

A Specific Learning Disability (SLD), or when more pervasive, (LD) is just that—*specific*—usually involving one or more learning weaknesses (e.g., reading, math) in an otherwise "normal" skills profile. It is, in some sense, a definition of *exclusion* because the child's school failure is NOT due to reduced intelligence, mental illness, or a sensory deficit of some sort. In fact, there may be no explanation at all for the "spiky" score profile we tend to see in these students, who make up about five percent of the school-aged population. Because SLD tends to co-occur with normal intelligence, kids with these disorders are well aware of their academic, and often, social, ineptness. Having taught teens with both LD and ID (Intellectual Disability; in my day, MR or "mental retardation"), I can verify the incredible difference in social perceptiveness that separates the two disability groups. My mentally young students with ID burst through the front door of the special education classroom with smiling faces, oblivious to social stigma; while those with LD slunk in the back way, sometimes well after the late bell had rung, and their nonhandicapped friends were safely out of visual range.

Being LD means *knowing* that you can't keep up with your peers in one or more academic areas, but not being able to correct the imbalance through extra effort or just plain hard work. As a result, the child with LD will often take extreme measures to hide his deficits from others. He may then adopt one or more of the following behavior problems designed to mask his deficits: stubborn refusal to do homework or in-class assignments; creating trouble or breaking class rules in order to avoid public embarrassment surrounding a test or spelling bee; becoming the "class clown" so as to gain social acceptance of non-LD peers; tattling on other classmates to call attention to their flaws and thereby "normalize" his own; school tardiness at the lower grades which leads to selective class cuts in junior high, truancy in high school, and eventual drop out.

## J.R. at Eighteen

Because I was brought into his case eight years into the appeal process, I didn't actually know J.R. at the time of his crime. Thus, in order to "meet him" and paint an accurate picture of his functional skills at age eighteen, I conducted a thorough search of all existing school and trial documents. Fortunately, the client's unusual background and longstanding special education enrollment yielded a sizeable paper trail that told a fairly complete story. School files are, in this sense, a sort of treasure chest, brimming with the first-hand observations of the client's teachers at a time when he was an innocent youth. As such, I relied heavily on teachers' statements in records and report cards, along with (unread) letters home, disciplinary write-ups, and the like, to form opinions about my clients' formative backgrounds.

Although J.R. was never described as a behavior problem by teachers, his dismal lack of academic progress was repeatedly noted. File entries enabled me to chart standardized test scores for reading, spelling, and math at three points during the now adult client's schooling. This profile presented a flat arrangement of lagging fourth-to-sixth-grade level skills that typify the embarrassment, failure, and defeat of many LD students. Little wonder that, after three grueling years of high school, J.R. dropped out altogether, preferring to wander the streets of Baton Rouge, hang out with buddies, and look for piecemeal employment.

By the time of his arrest the following year, this client's outlook was even less promising, as no academic progress had been made since he left elementary school. Indeed, standardized test scores included in the case file assembled after his 1994 arrest showed skills across the board stalled at fourth- and fifth-grade levels. This represented a slight decline from a junior high assessment which showed an ability to sound out individual printed words at a sixth-grade level; however, now, at age eighteen, this splinter skill had regressed by two years due to nonuse. In other words, J.R.'s avoidance of all school-related activities led to an even greater decline from his former reduced level of expertise.

In addition to continuing academic woes, J.R.'s language competence also lagged well behind age expectancy in young adulthood. I determined this by coding a language sample transcribed during his 1995 court testimony which yielded Readability Levels between grades three and four, and an accompanying Language Age of eight to ten years. A local psychologist hired that same year had eyeballed his current academic skills at ten-to-twelve year mental age levels, and estimated social maturity at age fourteen years. Finally, an undiagnosed attention deficit disorder (ADD) was evident in J.R.'s knee-jerk decision to act without a thorough plan plus his bumbling loss of focus during the robbery (described below) itself. It is therefore reasonable to conclude that, at age eighteen, the youth operated cognitively at the same level as a ten-to-fourteen-year-old child. This is even more probable in light of neurological research (Goldberg; National Institute on Mental Health, 2001) which found that the portions of the brain responsible for the "executive" decision-making that governs planning and oversight of one's own actions do not fully develop until the late teens or early twenties. Compound these research findings with others that document a two-to-four-year maturation lag in teens with cognitive disorders such as LD and ADD, and you get a better picture of just who J.R. was at the time of his crime. This is what happened.

**The Crime**

I have many times shared a saying of my colleague, Dr. Mark Cunningham, who now works out of Seattle: *"One boy is a boy; two boys make half a boy; and three boys—that's no boy at all."* He was referring to the "gang mentality" that takes over when a group of teenagers get together. In situations where teens have nothing constructive to do, that mentality can lead to mischief or outright crime. Indeed, studies of social psychology saw comparable, though passive, antisocial behavior in groups of adult city dwellers. In more than one of these studies, people would cross the street to avoid involvement in a crime scene or medical emergency. The thinking went something like, "It's not *my* responsibility—I could be hurting more than helping, so let someone else call 9-1-1." In both scenarios, active and passive "group think" overrides moral decision-making. For youths, it can lead to actions that one boy would never dream up, or be nervy enough to pull off, on his own.

So, now we return to J.R., a functionally illiterate school dropout who had failed to find employment for several months, hooking up with a like-minded peer to hatch a plan. Let me preface this by saying that the "plan" of one with learning and attention deficits is half-baked at best, and downright unworkable in most circumstances. This inability to connect the logistical dots leads most individuals with LD to pair up with, take orders from, or otherwise depend upon, friends they perceive as more competent to assist their executive decision-making. Little wonder that J.R. sought support from this fellow dropout. The pair then kicked around ideas that might facilitate the proposed robbery. Even so, the collaborative "plan" they came up with was sketchy as to time, place, victim, and the precise steps to use. Details didn't crystallize any further when J.R. obtained a handgun through this same acquaintance, but the acquisition did spur on a sudden decision to proceed with the robbery on his own.

In preparation, J.R. surveilled a convenience store on a major Baton Rouge thoroughfare to gauge its layout, plus the comings and goings of customers. Unfortunately, any useful information he had collected by watching the place neither influenced nor moderated his poorly-timed decision to carry out the robbery. Instead, he just showed up randomly, hung around for a bit, and then approached a lone workman sitting in his pickup truck in the middle of the almost empty parking lot. In choosing this particular victim on this day and at this time, J.R. didn't take into account any of the following variables: First, the proposed hold-up would take place in broad daylight and in a parking lot clearly visible to traffic on the busy adjacent street. Second, the proposed victim was, quite obviously, a low-income laborer who was unlikely to carry much money, either on his person or inside the truck. Third, J.R. had not thought of a plausible excuse to approach the man and therefore had to "wing it" at the last minute, with disastrous results. Fourth, because he thought concretely like a much younger child, this eighteen-year-old had only envisioned a single outcome: his own; i.e., a quick, easy transfer of money and a clean getaway. The youth was therefore totally unprepared to adapt to novel, changing, and/or unforeseen circumstances, thus panicked when things began to go wrong.

One more thing that J.R. had not taken into account was the body style of the victim's old truck. Here he encountered, for the first time, the sort of running boards that help drivers and passengers access the raised level of the cab. It was there that the teenager decided to begin his approach, so he mounted the running board adjacent to the driver's window. The workman looked up from his lunch and was somewhat surprised to see someone standing just outside, so he rolled down the truck window. J.R. then realized that he had not planned any sort of conversational opener. He fumbled for a few seconds, then impulsively asked to bum a cigarette. This was, in itself, rather odd in that J.R. a) didn't smoke, and b) didn't have a match or lighter. Accordingly, once given the cigarette, he had to ask for help lighting it. By now the driver must have realized that something was definitely "up" and adjusted his demeanor just enough that it fueled J.R.'s growing panic. J.R. pulled the gun out of his pocket and demanded the driver hand over all his money. This is not the first time that one of my LD clients drew a weapon *after* interacting casually with his victim. In another case, a youth named Mark simultaneously donned a ski mask—*in front of the victim*—and declared his real intention. Was it an afterthought, that "one second" bad decision that Tom spoke of, or just a frantic adaptation to the surprises that almost always pop up when a "human" variable enters the equation? Maybe it was all of these.

What happened next was anything but "premeditated" and, reportedly, surprised the would-be robber as much as it did the victim: J.R.'s foot suddenly slipped off the running board and, as he flailed to right himself, the gun went off in random fashion. Tragically, the bullet was a direct hit, and the truck driver was dead within moments. This was that "one second" where everything went disastrously wrong, changing several lives forever. Passersby heard the shot, saw J.R. running away, and called police to the scene. The youth was apprehended without incident within a few blocks of the convenience store.

### Arrest and Trial

Police in major cities have been highly trained in interrogation techniques that work quite well on most people, and are even more effective with the disabled. When one of these techniques is employed to the letter, I've seen *completely innocent* defendants admit to wrongdoing. Some of these hapless individuals become overwhelmed by the logical presentation of their community heroes ("If the policeman says I did it, then I must have"); while others "confess" to please the "good cop," or simply to get a Coke. Most people have seen this and similar techniques in action on television via the many "cop shows" that have cycled through the top ten prime time listings. Here's a typical interrogation scenario.

Effective techniques usually team up two officers—one friendly and the other adversarial—who take turns questioning the defendant with one singular objective in mind: to get a confession. Usually, the "bad cop" applies increasing pressure to come clean, often while withholding food and drink. Since outright lies are not out of bounds during a police interrogation, the bad cop often dangles false proof of guilt as he continues to badger the defendant over several hours time. At that point, the "good cop" takes over, offering protection from his partner's growing intensity, understanding how *tough* it must be, and even supplying excuses for the actions that led to the crime. For example, the good cop may suggest the defendant's actions were accidental, or that victims sometimes "deserve it." He usually ends with a kindly lecture about how "being a man" means taking responsibility, and finally suggests that owning up to it "right now" will help the defendant gain leniency later on in court. "This is your chance to tell your side of the story" is a typical offer that seems to work well with defendants of limited intellect. So do offers to speak to the judge on his behalf, lies about existing evidence (videotapes, blood, fingerprints, a codefendant's confession) that already incriminates him, and threats of abandonment if he doesn't cooperate immediately.

But officers don't have to be specially trained to take full advantage of a learning and language disabled client like J.R. The pair in question had him singing like a bird within a couple of hours and locked securely away by supper. J.R.'s biggest fear at that point was trying to get someone to notify his nonlingual mother of his whereabouts so she wouldn't worry too much. An overworked public defender was hastily appointed so that the trial could swiftly proceed.

The all-white jury chosen by both lawyers in the case didn't waste much time in the guilt (a "done deal") or punishment phases of J.R.'s trial, quickly rendering a death verdict that hardly surprised anyone. This, despite the fact that, encountering ongoing communication problems in his client, the public defender had gone to the trouble to appoint a local psychologist to examine J.R., and that her report had been introduced at trial. Here, test data collected at age eighteen revealed a verbal IQ in the low 80s along with academic skills stalled at elementary school levels. This report verified that, post high school, J.R. was not appreciably different from the ten-year-old youth who was exited from speech therapy and forced into the mainstream of life. But numbers like these mean little to unsophisticated country folk who may themselves suffer similar deficits. In fact, it has been my personal finding that many such jurors recall "Grandpa" or "Mr. Hicks at the general store" as functioning similarly and therefore minimize, or totally negate, the functional impact of mild to moderate disabilities on behavior. Accordingly, the bus to Angola Prison was gassed up and ready to transport J.R. to Death Row before nightfall on the day of the verdict.

## Time on Death Row

There's one amazing thing about J.R. that nobody ever suspected prior to his incarceration: He could absorb academic skills and material like a veritable sponge by applying heroic effort under perfect (focused, sustained) conditions. Let me first point out that, depending on the routine and policies of the particular prison, Death Row generally provides a rather isolated existence with little to do other than read. This may be why J.R. quickly realized that, if only to break the boredom of his new daily life, he had better improve his skills through self-study. I have often mused about how effective isolated study tends to be in self-improvement efforts, and can only imagine how that may be magnified if an appropriate teacher were thrown into the mix. But, we can't lock up our LD students in order to secure better focus and commitment to the learning task. Teachers therefore have to compete with all the social distractions teens face both in and out of the classroom, and can only hope that discrete pieces of daily instruction will link together to yield academic progress.

So, here we have J.R., bored to (forgive the expression) death for eight years, with nothing to do but focus on self-improvement. To do this, he accessed self-study materials through the prison library along with certain outside sources and proceeded to set up a rigorous daily schedule that looked something like this:

| | |
|---|---|
| 6:00-7:00: | Morning Exercise and Weight Training |
| 7:00: | Breakfast |
| 8:00-12:00: | Reading and Composition |
| 12:00: | Lunch |
| 1:00-3:00: | Content Reading (e.g., History) with Note Taking |
| 3:00-5:00: | Academic and Personal Journaling |
| 5:00: | Dinner |
| 6:00-8:00: | Current Events (via TV) |

What impressed me the most was the final two hours of "current events" tacked on to J.R.'s long day of self-study, an addition which made him far more informed than myself about world, national, and local news. Imagine eight years of adherence to this rigorous schedule, and you will have a glimpse of the twenty-six-year-old man I encountered at Angola Prison in 2002. This new and improved J.R. had already earned a GED high school diploma and was beginning to pursue his AA degree through courses offered online.

### J.R. at Twenty-Six

Marie and I were finally admitted to the interior of Angola's Death Row and escorted to a pleasant, though windowless, room used by staff and certain inmates (helpers called "trustees") for "breaks." Fortunately, both groups honored our court-ordered request for privacy, so only the most minimal interruptions occurred throughout the six-hour assessment. Marie made introductions, chatted with J.R. about his case for a bit, and then left us alone. Here's the J.R. that I encountered.

Since no amount of studying can alter inborn intelligence, J.R.'s composite IQ score in the low-average range came as no surprise. My only intention in measuring it was to provide the comparison point for computing Specific Learning Disabilities, should they still be present. Happily, they were not. Instead, significant gains in the academic areas of reading and spelling verified this diligent client's newfound ability to comprehend most adult material. Now improved to a twelfth-grade level, these two areas in particular had benefitted greatly from J.R.'s current structured study program, where he read, referenced, and then reread materials as many as three times to insure accurate interpretation of communicative intent. Recently completed books included biographies, texts, and religious novels. Accordingly, the client's fund of so-called "basic information" demonstrated age-appropriate (adult) development due to the what can only be described as voracious reading over the past eight years.

In contrast, J.R.'s math skills had only advanced two and one-half years (to a seventh-grade level) since last tested in adolescence. This was not very surprising, in that few people do math problems just for fun in their spare time. This is one area that was projected to improve given proper instructional opportunities via the visiting "tutor" program that was being instituted at the prison. Neither did social knowledge improve past a fifteen-year level via his solitary, self-guided study activities. The good news was that even these slightly lagging subskills would no longer qualify as formal Learning Disabilities using the standard computation formula.

On the negative side of the equation, J.R. repeatedly demonstrated "holes" in academic content gleaned without the guidance of a teacher and/or opportunities for practice in community contexts. In addition, his auditory information processing remained at junior high school levels, and he demonstrated a form of ADD that presented as delayed response time when attending to cognitive tasks. Charted, his function across tested skills still depicted the irregular ("spiky") profile of a person who suffers deficits in specific cognitive processes.

Finally, it came as no surprise that J.R.'s processing and expression of oral language remained moderately reduced. This was due primarily to severe language deprivation in early childhood, and now compounded by eight years living essentially alone. Accordingly, self-expression scored almost four years below his ability to understand the language of others. Expressive errors observed throughout testing verified continuing mild to moderate deficits in the scan and retrieval process needed for more automatic word retrieval. Several of his answers to vocabulary test items were therefore restricted to only vague associations from recent reading. For example, asked to label a test plate depicting a *pillar or column*, J.R. only knew that it might have "something to do with Corinthians." Several of the other pictured items were incorrectly approximated due to non-use. In these instances, J.R. had *read* the words, but had never actually used them in conversation.

Language immaturity noted at several points in our interaction demonstrated that, even in adulthood, J.R. was not entirely appropriate in two-directional social conversation. For example, when I inquired as to the source of noise which came from behind one wall of the testing room, my question ("What's behind this wall?") required a descriptive answer such as, "The mess hall." However, J.R.'s answer, "The other side," demonstrates the concreteness of a child. Though it did answer my basic question, his response cannot be characterized as *communicating* the content necessary to satisfy the needs of the questioner; that is, no noise source was named. This example illustrates the sort of social disconnect that can be seen in the adult language of children with impoverished beginnings.

In the final analysis, even though J.R.'s early speech/language therapy must be judged "successful" in correcting certain mechanical deficits, a pragmatic (social) detachment was still noted that occasionally derailed interactive conversation. Now, as an adult, he still required additional time to reflect upon, encode, and perfect his responses in complex situations, a factor which should not have been overlooked by attorneys in analyzing the events that led to the crime. It seems imperative to add that, at the age of eighteen, his language and processing capabilities were *far less developed* than what I measured in J.R. some eight years later. This updated assessment presented test data and historical comparisons that helped to explain the immaturity of the youth who dreamed up an armed robbery in broad daylight in a busy Baton Rouge location. His ongoing inaccuracy under rushed, high-stimulus conditions also helped to explain the end result.

Unfortunately, these findings were not fully presented during J.R.'s 1995 trial, other than in footnote format. The connection between Learning Disability and poor adaptive decision-making was not clarified, nor the social neediness of many such youngsters which leads to their easy manipulation by more competent peers. Had the jury known something about the daily struggles of Learning Disabled children and their enduring social frustration and embarrassment, their developmental lags that persist into young adulthood, their need for external coaching and tendency to bumble matters without it, they may have reached a different decision regarding culpability and punishment in this matter—at least this was our argument to the Court in J.R.'s post-conviction trial.

## Appeal and Case Outcome

It took several more years for J.R.'s *habeas* case to appear before a judge in a Baton Rouge courtroom. By then, he was represented by highly competent lawyers from firms in New Orleans and Houston; but sadly, Marie, his original guardian angel, had passed away from brain cancer. While she watched from above, I was called to present his historical and current test findings, along with information regarding Learning Disabilities as a syndrome and the effects of early language deprivation. I was pleased beyond measure when, over the state's objection, the judge allowed me to introduce a PowerPoint presentation in order to provide full and detailed explanations. It was just like teaching a college class, but with a lot more on the line than grades on a transcript.

✧ ✧ ✧

Would I even be writing this if the outcome wasn't somewhat wonderful? No indeed. But rather than tell you what happened, let me simply quote the email I received from the lead attorney when the case was fully resolved:

Nancy –

*I wanted to let you know that we have finally resolved the J.R. post-conviction case. After we concluded the presentation of our case in chief, the State asked for a substantial delay to consider and prepare its case. During that delay, and in no small part due to your tremendous testimony, the State raised the possibility of a compromise. It took several rounds of offers and counters to get to an agreeable compromise, but we got there. This past Friday, Judge J. approved a deal that allowed J.R. to enter a plea to second degree murder and a life sentence. He returned to Angola that day to spend his first night off Death Row in more than sixteen years.*

*During those sixteen years, J.R. became the only Death Row inmate in the long history of the Louisiana State Penitentiary to obtain his GED. He has now completed thirty hours of college coursework towards a Bachelor of Criminal Justice at [name withheld] State University. Given these accomplishments, the Assistant Warden for Programming offered J.R. a job as a GED tutor!*

*The result could not have been obtained without your stellar work on the case. And I have to say that I have never presented a more effective witness in any court. It was an honor to work with you.*

*[We] hope to be able to get the entire team together for a celebratory dinner in New Orleans in the near future and we do hope you can attend.*

*All the best,*
*Attorney, MDR, Houston, Texas*

So, there you have it: a heartwarming, ego-boosting (sorry about that; just quoting), happy ending indeed. But no dinner. I recently called the lead attorney to obtain his permission to quote this email and was told he still keeps in contact with J.R., who's doing quite well. Certainly, serving a life prison sentence would never be self-chosen, but it sure beats Death Row. Another positive note here is the fact that GED tutors enjoy higher status among inmates along with occasional "payment" in the form of soup, cigarettes, favors, "protection," and other desirable goods. All things considered, I can't think of a better ending to a lengthy journey toward justice. As I stated at the beginning of this chapter, J.R.'s was the single most rewarding case in my career as a forensic assessor.

# CHAPTER TWO
# James, a Story of Perseveration

James' short-lived criminal career was so bumbling and pathetic that people have a hard time believing it. Maybe that's why the details of his case have remained crystal clear in my mind for twenty years. Here is James' story.

## Background

James was a large, lumbering thirty-six-year-old not unlike the "Lennie" character in *Of Mice and Men*. Over six feet tall and weighing in around three hundred pounds, he looked like a force to be reckoned with. But James was truly a "gentle giant" who, due to moderate learning and attention disorders, often depended upon his brother, Sam, for guidance and protection. He lived in a trailer behind his brother's house and, having never passed the test for a driver's license, used only a bicycle to get around town. Sam owned a plumbing business which he worked alone, with the exception of times when he needed James' brute strength to yank out a toilet or sink. This was one of those times, so James accompanied Sam that morning to the home of a single woman whose bathroom was being remodeled.

Since "Norma" worked as a teacher, she had given Sam her house key which he kept inside his plumbing truck, hanging on a hook alongside those of his other customers.

Sam and James let themselves in the side door of the home which opened directly into the woman's kitchen. They then proceeded to the bathroom all the way at the end of a center hall corridor. James took note of two bedrooms located on either side of the hallway. When the plumbing job was completed for the day, the brothers cleaned up the area, relocked the house, and returned to the truck, where Sam replaced the woman's key on its hook. Since the plumbing job was nearing completion, James didn't have the time or wherewithal to think through the idea hatching in his mind. It instead became the sort of "half-plan" introduced in J.R.'s previous chapter. His "plan" went something like this: steal the key out of the truck, bike over to the woman's house, go in the side door, take valuable items, and leave before she gets back from work.

Since Sam was not scheduled to work on that particular plumbing job the following day, James decided that it was now or never. He went out to the truck before 9:00 A.M., the time his brother typically left for work, entered it, and pocketed the woman's key. He then put a roll of duct tape and fourteen trash bags—that's *fourteen* of the giant plastic bags that line standard size garbage cans—in his bike basket and pedaled down the road to crime.

Things began well: Norma had already left for work and the key easily opened the side door. James dropped his supplies in the kitchen, took the first of the trash bags, and began going through the various rooms of the house in search of things to steal. This is where his plan got sidetracked. Time rolled by as he riffled through the contents of virtually every drawer, closet, bin, and cabinet, stuffing any and everything that appealed to him inside the bags. As each bag filled, he took it back to the kitchen, sealed the top opening with duct tape, and added it to the growing pile by the side door. When police detectives later opened the bags James left behind in his hasty exit, they found quirky, unrelated items with no apparent use or resale value—cat toys, potpourri, a defunct transistor radio, and an old fever thermometer were only a few of the highlights.

Hours ticked by as James perseverated over filling up the trash bags. Looking at my later test results, it's easy to imagine his ADD kicking in at some point, rendering him floundering and directionless in the process. He not only lost track of time, but also failed to think about how he would get all of this loot home *while riding a bicycle*. Juggling only one or two of the giant bags would be quite a feat, but he now had seven of them piled up by the kitchen door. Stepping over and around the bags, he had steadied himself by grabbing nearby appliances, leaving ample fingerprint evidence virtually everywhere.

As the afternoon marched on, James had worked his way to the very back of the house, filling what appeared to be his eighth trash bag with random items. That was when the woman returned home from her day at work.

It appeared that Norma entered the house using the front door and started back toward the bedroom area. She stopped short, however, upon seeing a few dropped items in the hallway. That was probably when she heard intermittent muted sounds coming from the back bedroom and saw the pile of bulging trash bags in the kitchen to her left. Her scream of surprise was James' first inkling that he had a big and unexpected problem on his hands.

James emerged from the bedroom with the intention to quickly flee from the house; however, Norma now stood in the hallway, blocking his only exit. He nevertheless decided to make a run for it, knocking the small woman to the floor with all three hundred pounds of his body weight. To James' horror, he had inadvertently crushed her larynx in the collision and she now lay dying in front of him. He therefore took a heavy ashtray from the trash bag in his hand and rendered her unconscious. Watching James' tearful videotaped confession, I couldn't help but think of my disabled student E.J. who made a similar effort to relieve suffering when he mistakenly dropped a hoe on one of the many kittens hanging around his yard. E.J. loved animals and couldn't stand to see one suffer, so he dug a hole and quickly buried the dying kitten inside. This incident came back to me when I heard James' tearful confession in his subsequent videotaped police interview.

My previous comment that James was known around town as a "gentle giant" was actually quite an accurate representation. As a result, he was horrified at what had unfolded at the woman's house and wandered around despondently for days afterward. It didn't take more than that for the police to come calling. They picked up James without incident. A harmonica from the victim's house was still inside his jacket pocket. No special questioning technique was needed to exact a confession from the remorseful client, who sat crying and rocking back and forth on his chair saying, "Just kill me ... just kill me." The D.A. complied by opting to seek the death penalty. That was when James' public defender called me into the case.

## Assessment

File review revealed that James had attended special education classes throughout his school experience, where he was enrolled in a Special Day Class (SDC) for Educationally Handicapped students. The earliest school records available described him as "restless" with a short attention span for academic work. Several psycho-stimulant medications were tested before settling on a combination of Dexedrine and Thorazine to remedy his attention problems. Indeed, it appears to have been his medical doctor who initiated James' first special education referral.

Notes from the client's twelfth grade IEP (a school-based diagnosis and planning team) meeting verify continued enrollment in the SDC with "0 minutes mainstreamed" into the regular class program. This means that the team members found no skills developed to the point that he could compete in the regular classroom. At the end of that year, the school district granted James a diploma using the "differential standard" allowable for special education students. No longer applied to my knowledge, the standard allowed kids with special needs to skip the usual academic competency testing required for typical students. James therefore merely "aged out" of school based on his good attendance record.

My four-hour assessment of this client yielded the following skills profile:

- An IQ in the low-average range, with better nonverbal than verbal subskills;
- Second to fifth grade academic skills, with borderline to clear qualification as Specific Learning Disabilities;
- Information processing skills hovering at seven-to-ten year age levels with spiky highs and lows depending on the particular tasks involved;
- Language skills at eleven to twelve-year age levels;
- Severe attention deficits marked by slowed response time, high variability, and extreme omissions that were consistent with a continued ADD diagnosis. These errors were severe enough that the test protocol recommended neurological testing to rule out organic causation.

My report ended with a research review of so-called "susceptibility factors" that place people with Learning Disabilities at greater risk of one day falling into the criminal justice system. These include 1) making poor initial decisions that can lead to unintended crimes; 2) being unable to make adjustments that might abort impending trouble once actions were underway; 3) getting caught more easily; and 4) being ineffective self-advocates at arrest. Specific contributing behaviors referred to in these studies were things like impulsivity (described as fast bad decisions under stress), poor planning skills, the need for external coaching to regulate one's own actions, and an inability to foresee logical consequences of proposed actions. In James' case, these and other problems were combined with raging, untreated ADD, producing a perfect combination for failure.

## Trial and Outcome

At trial, James' defense attorney went through my various test findings to establish a factual basis for claims as to his disabling conditions. His brother also testified, as did a few friends, mostly as witnesses to his previously good character and amiable demeanor. Having already confessed on videotape, James was quickly found guilty of the murder and now faced a penalty phase to determine a life sentence versus the death penalty. The jury listened to all of the evidence and opted for life.

There's no moral to this story and no happy ending. A woman is dead because of an inept crime gone horribly wrong. The man responsible is confined to prison, possibly for the rest of his life. Even if parole were a possibility, it is highly unlikely that James could ever qualify. That's because parole is granted very seldom in California and when it is, it's because the inmate has jumped three important hurdles: 1) he has "programmed well" by earning a diploma or vocational certification and has no disciplinary write-ups; 2) he demonstrates appropriate "insight and remorse" for his crime; and 3) he has adequate parole plans in place for home, job, and community support after release. So let's take these requirements apart with James' particular skill set in mind.

## Meeting Parole Requirements

To begin with, James is unlikely to "program well," because his learning and attentional difficulties will tend to undermine the completion of any formal education or training classes. He already has a high school "diploma" of sorts, and has no need to reinvent that wheel while in custody. That leaves the vocational options, most of which require high school level academic skills for inclusion. Just why this is so remains a mystery to me because many or most of the trades taught in prison classes require very little reading and are thus well suited to inmates who are "visual" or "hands-on" learners. People like this, and that includes *most* students with Learning Disabilities, pick things up by watching and doing rather than by reading and listening. Accordingly, I and other disability advocates have made recommendations that the prison system ditch the academic prerequisites for trades where related skills are not essential.

Second, while James was very, *very* sorry for what happened, true *insight* is unlikely because this condition requires a deep, thorough, and mature understanding of all of the factors concerned. Webster's Dictionary defines *insight* as "the power to see what is not evident to the average mind," and goes on to say that insight requires one to go beyond obvious or superficial factors, applying clarity of focus and "keen judgment" to a given situation. By the very nature of their disabilities, my students and clients do not have "average minds" and are largely incapable of cognitive processes involving mental maturity, clear focus, and keen judgment. They may be able to offer simple explanations of where and how they went wrong but, much like younger children, that is the limit of their cognitive capacity. Instead, they tend to see things only from their own limited perspective, and fail to generalize this more broadly so as to develop the capacity to "discern sympathy for others" that true *insight* demands.

The final hurdle requiring adequate parole plans is the one James would have the best chance of clearing, but only if his family and community would agree to welcome and care for him once released. Here, he would have to show proof of a secure residence, plans for re-entry counseling, and a potential job offer, at minimum. Would an angry community allow this? Would a brother who was essentially "duped" be able to forgive and forget? Would he ever look at James again without remembering the tragic death and his own unwitting role in the circumstances that contributed to it? Maybe so, but making all of these arrangements from a prison cell is difficult for anyone, and nearly impossible for inmates with limited capabilities.

Of course, all of this assumes that parole is even a possibility for James. If instead, he was granted life without the possibility of parole, the hurdles I've described above remain a moot point. Nevertheless, for other inmates with disabilities, obtaining parole remains only a remote possibility because achieving it presents a triple whammy they are unlikely to overcome.

# CHAPTER THREE
## Carl, Disorganization and Impulsivity

Over the past several decades, cases of diagnosed attention disorders (usually referred to as ADD or ADHD) and related information processing problems appear to have increased in frequency, not only in the general population, but among criminal defendants. Accordingly, many of those who found their way into my caseload exhibited attentional disorders as their primary or secondary diagnoses. I might add here that when a person has more than one disability, the more debilitating of the two dictates his or her primary classification. So, a child labeled LD/ADD suffers primarily from a Learning Disability which limits academic growth, with Attention Deficit Disorder identified as a contributing factor. Since this is a very common combination, I am including attention deficits in Part One of this book, designated for Learning Disabilities, along with related language-based disorders. Nevertheless, it's certainly possible to have an attention disorder that exists on its own and is not accompanied by learning problems, especially if the individual is "smart" to begin with. In this situation, it's hard to call the individual "disabled" in the standard sense, because this "difference" has no apparent negative impact on his life. Or does it?

## What is ADD/ADHD?

Most of us can only imagine what it would be like to repeatedly cycle in and out of focus and have to consciously reengage in tasks throughout the day. This scenario describes a true Attention *Deficit* Disorder which can create gaps in academic, as well as social information. That's because omissions during periods of inattention result in inaccurate mental filling and storage of content and, ultimately, errors at recall. So, even where ADD exists in isolation, the individual must remain on "hyper-alert" to prompt his own attention, identify what he just missed, and fill in content gaps. Most people with ADD simply cannot maintain these exhausting adjustments on a continuing basis in everyday life. So, you can be sure that successful people who report overcoming their attention deficits to reach the top have had to expend a great deal of extra effort to get there.

The disorders that fall under this broad umbrella can have different behavioral effects. I'm reminded of a story told by the director of a private school for children with learning and attention deficits. The new multi-purpose room had just been completed with one minor, but potentially disastrous, error: the light switch had been placed right next to a fire alarm call box. So, the director assembled all of the students in the new room for a heads-up warning about being careful, etc. A week later the first alarm went off and little Jimmy was called into the director's office where he was administered a lecture about the dangers of wasting the firemen's time with a false alarm should a real fire pop up across town. Trying to engage distractible Jimmy, the director purposely used exaggerated arm gestures to drive home the point that calling firemen HERE could lead to disaster OVER THERE ... when Jimmy, attention rooted on the dramatic arm gestures, suddenly blurts out, "My father has a watch just like that one!" This kid has no *deficit* of attention—he pays attention to *everything* at once. Accordingly, his problem is to screen out extraneous distractors so as to focus on the task at hand (or arm as the case may be).

## Detecting and Describing Attentional Deficits

Assessing any client with ADD or ADHD should include a thorough review of school and medical records, along with a detailed analysis of all of the variables of attention described below. A description of everyday functioning must then focus on the client's information processing capabilities to determine any "breakdowns" that occur during the intake, organization, storage, retrieval, and/or self-expression phases. As noted above, a true attention *deficit* tends to interfere with initial intake, creating content errors that manifest throughout the rest of the processing chain. In other words, not paying attention up front is likely to have a "cascade-effect" during the remaining processing tasks. Likewise, distractibility mid-task can lead to "holes" in learned content.

Many clinicians diagnose attention deficits by comparing observed and/or reported behavior with a checklist of symptoms referenced in professional handbooks. I found this method to be imprecise and, frankly, useless in describing a client's functioning over time and under varying task conditions. Neither does it explain the fact that many children with diagnosed ADD/ADHD who demonstrate problems attending to even short-term classroom tasks, can sit for hours playing self-chosen video games at home. Accordingly, to conduct a more precise measure of attention, I came to rely upon a computerized test* that separates out and defines the specific variables of attention as follows:

> *<u>Omissions</u> of attention result from intermittent lapses in vigilance over the length of a task. Omissions tend to produce a pattern of cycling attention which, in turn, results in spotty knowledge, incomplete intake of directions and/or information, and partial learning of academic content. Omissions are the most recognized component of isolated ADD (without hyperactivity).*

*Commissions are false positives associated with impulsive and/or random behavior. This dimension describes an individual's ability to inhibit himself and his physical actions. High Commissions usually involve random, purposeless, or "knee-jerk" reactions which seem to be outside the physical control of the individual. Commissions are typical errors in subjects identified as having the "H" (hyperactivity) component of ADHD.*

*Reaction Time is simply the amount of time it takes for a person to formulate and produce responses on demand. This variable is measured over task conditions which change from low-stimulus ("boring," infrequent appearance of targets) to high-stimulus (very frequent targets that require heightened vigilance) conditions.*

*Variability refers to the consistency of speed and accuracy across time and test conditions. As such, this measure helps to explain changes in the frequency of Omissions and Commissions in test subjects, as well as their inconsistency in carrying out tasks.*

What I want to stress here is that attentional deviations are not confined to simple lapses of vigilance, but also involve poor impulse control, slowed reactions, and inconsistency over time.

### Precision Measurement of Attentional Disorders

The in-depth computer-based test that I preferred runs for twenty-two grueling minutes divided into two equal halves, the first of which is a "low-stimulus" condition. Here, small white dots ("blips") are presented on the dark screen at two-second intervals in an infrequent and random pattern. The test subject must maintain consistent attention, pressing the button on a hand-held microswitch whenever the blips occur.

Sound familiar? Well, it should, because the test was derived from and mimics the same task undertaken by radar operators detecting enemy ships at sea. The "boring" nature of the Half 1 task demands sustained vigilance which is challenging for even these highly-trained professionals, and practically impossible for children and adults with true attention deficits.

As the twelve-minute mark nears, visual blips on the screen increase to become almost constant, with random non-targets (no blip) as exceptions. Eleven minutes of consistent accuracy here is pure torture for people who suffer from the "impulsivity" associated with ADHD. Instead, they make any number of "false positives" (defined as Commissions, above), which cause extreme frustration when self-detected. In fact, it is fairly common for these test subjects to react physically (flinching, smacking the table) and/or verbally (shocked exclamations, swearing) at the onset of Half 2, then lapse into a sort of comatose state of surrender as the test continues.

How a person's speed of response varies over time and across the two test conditions is also important to accurately describe his or her attention deficit condition. A diligent test subject will typically slow somewhat as Half 2 gets underway so as to avoid false positives, and will maintain some level of caution until the end. As long as the speed of response is not *inordinately* slow, this is considered a good accommodation for the high-stress task. Of particular interest here is the subject who does not slow at all, but races on at a fast speed, making random, usually blind, commission errors. Is he just faking the test? To know this, we can check the calculated Reliability Score, a sort of "lie factor" built into the assessment.

A subject's variability (consistency) over time and across the two test halves is the final consideration in accurately describing his or her attentional capabilities. How cautious does he have to be to maintain accuracy? Is he able to relax into a more "automatic" response style once familiarity with each test half is achieved? If not, what is the price he pays for accuracy in terms of personal consistency?

All four variables—Omissions, Commissions, Response Time, and Variability—are analyzed throughout the test to produce a print-out of deviation scores from what is considered "normal" for the age of the subject. It also computes an "ADD Score" based on particular data tracked during the full test. With any luck, these results will demonstrate *exactly* where an individual's problems occur. For example, a client with very high Omissions but a good Commissions score suffers from cyclic lapses of attention. Are they worse when "bored" (Half 1) or when highly stimulated (Half 2)? Test data help in making these determinations. Conversely, a person with low Omissions and high Commissions has problems with self-inhibition (impulsivity). How long and under what conditions can he maintain self control? Perhaps he begins well and is able to maintain control for the first eleven minutes, or even longer, then becomes random and imprecise. Or, maybe a mixed error pattern occurs depending on high versus low stimulation. All of this is knowable if the right test is administered, and backed up with records review, parent and self-reports, and results from information processing tests in the complete battery. Having now provided this foundational explanation of ADD/ADHD, let me present the story of Carl.

### Criminal Case

On the surface, Carl's case looked like a lost cause, even from the most optimistic defense attorney's perspective. This attractive, biracial twenty-two-year-old had been a basketball star throughout his school career and was never enrolled in special education classes. Although teachers and coaches recalled many behaviors consistent with ADD/ ADHD, the family had refused medical intervention in the form of drug therapy for the condition. That was because Carl's mother, a nurse, was aware that poor appetite, stunted growth, and insomnia were common side effects of many popular "ADD drugs," especially in children.

When I entered the case, Carl had already been found guilty of the robbery-murder of a convenience store cashier and now faced the death penalty. As the lone assailant, all of his actions were video and audiotaped via store surveillance equipment. Here, Carl can be seen entering the high-stimulus environment of a small convenience store and approaching the cluttered counter where he attempts to purchase cigarettes. While waiting, he alternately stares at the counter and at another uncluttered surface, presumably in order to gather his wits and proceed with the robbery. He then orders the cashier onto the floor, face down, while he empties money from the register. At this point, Carl steps out of camera range, but can be clearly heard demanding repeatedly that the clerk remain still and stop scooting around on the floor. Here, the clerk was apparently trying to reach a "panic button" installed on the back side of the counter which would summon the police. After several pleas to stay still, two shots are heard, followed by Carl's final comment before fleeing: "*Stupid m—f—.*"

## Assessment Results

Carl's ADD condition was clearly observable in the various jail settings I accessed for his three-day assessment. For example, only minimal distractibility was observed when he was tested in a private cubicle facing a blank wall on Day 1; but he fell apart completely when seated at an interview "counter" in the main attorney room on Day 2. In this setting, Carl was observed to scatter his focus to any and all external stimuli, with particular difficulties whenever any visual distractions occurred. Since he faced an entry door with much inmate and guard activity, these distractions were considerable. The result was that Carl remained virtually untestable in this highly charged Day 2 setting. Accordingly, Day 3 was arranged in a private office inside the medical unit of the jail where only minimal outside distracters could reduce his concentration. Yet, even here, Carl got sidetracked by any movement outside the room's small window, and thus required repeated redirection to task. He also needed extra help "transitioning" to new tasks, following breaks, and even where significant shifts in body position occurred. Finally, when a gnat entered the test area, he could not focus on tasks until it was eliminated. With distractibility of this magnitude, in-depth assessment of attention became a necessary addition to the test battery.

Carl was first administered a composite IQ test to establish a comparison point for computing Specific Learning Disabilities, if present. Here, he scored at only 80 in the verbal portion, but at 99 in the nonverbal subtest. This calculates a composite (combined) IQ in the low-average range which does not represent either his below-average verbal, or his average performance skills. It should be pointed out that, in some states, this nineteen-point discrepancy would be enough to qualify a student as an "IWEN" (Individual With Exceptional Needs). Not so for Carl, however, who apparently relied on his better nonverbal skills to achieve junior high level academic skills that satisfied the commonly applied "literacy standard" needed for adult competence. Additional mild skill reductions in information processing and language also fell in line with Carl's verbal and composite IQ scores, and thus failed to compute the "significant" discrepancy (a twenty-two point spread) that defines a Specific Learning Disability. It should nevertheless be noted that it took Carl twelve years of schooling to learn roughly seven years of material. This means that he mastered approximately 58%, *but missed 42% of the content* due to continuing attentional deficits.

This evaluation included interviews with two of Carl's former basketball coaches to gauge the everyday effects of his observed ADD condition. Here, Coach A recalled personal inconsistency, along with situational inattentiveness, as behavioral norms. He added that "something interfered with [Carl's] ability to make good decisions" and that he had "special problems and needs" that were not always addressed in school programs. As a result, the youth was "not a very good student" who struggled to keep his grades at acceptable levels in order to play ball. This coach admitted times when he influenced teachers to raise Carl's grades so his GPA was good enough to stay on the team. Despite occasional frustration in trying to reach the boy, Coach A's special interest resulted in genuine affection between the two and the formation of a mentor relationship. Coach B, who served as assistant basketball coach, recalled becoming so concerned about Carl's wandering attention that he contacted the high school guidance counselor to recommend placement in a program for "at risk kids." This advice apparently remained unheeded by all concerned.

What I found most interesting in the above statements was Coach A's remark that "something" interfered with consistency and decision-making in this youth. It appears from data derived in my subsequent assessment that this nebulous "something" had everything to do with Carl's undiagnosed and untreated ADD. Indeed, casual observations were all the Coach needed to ascertain that something was "odd about how his mind functions" not only in academic, but also social and recreational settings. Consequently, it was not surprising to learn that Carl had intermittent lapses in focus while on the basketball court as well as during instructional time-outs. Whenever he became distracted during a time-out, one coach or the other would prompt the youngster's attention by calling his name or "grabbing his arm." Even so, Carl seemed to tune out some of the information provided to his team. In this regard, Coach A recalled numerous instances where he would set up a play during a time-out and send the team back out on the floor, only to find Carl out of position or otherwise unprepared to do his part. Teammates would then have to remind Carl of his position so that he could be successful the next time they rebounded the ball. Coaches and players came to expect that the otherwise gifted player "would have to go through and screw it up once" before he could transition to the new play. As the head Coach summarized, "It always took one time."

## Carl's Attention Deficit Disorder

Carl was administered the computer-based test described above in order to obtain hard data that would determine his qualification as one with a true Attention Deficit Disorder (ADD). These test results are reported as *Standard Deviations* and *Standard Scores*, both of which require brief definition. Standard Deviations (SDs) are actually scoring bands, typically fifteen points each, above and below the mid-point of a particular test. The Standard Scores that accompany SDs are like mini-IQs with a population average of 100. Accordingly, one SD below the mean yields a Standard Score of 85 which falls precisely on the borderline separating "low-normal" from "below average" population bands. Minus two SD bands would equate to a Standard Score of only 70, which is clearly sub-average. Knowing this will help to clarify the deficits in Carl's performance profile, where Commissions (impulsivity), alone, scored in the average range (Standard Score of 106).

In contrast, Carl's scores for both Omissions (inattention) and Variability plunged more than five Standard Deviations below the norm, computing Standard Scores so low as to be unmeasurable (below 25). The final variable of attention, Response Time, was very slow (-4.74 Standard Deviations), earning a Standard Score of only 28. These extreme deviations identified a severe enough attention deficit condition to "warrant consideration of (drug) treatment," per the printout. The analysis further recommended a neurological or neuropsychiatric workup due to the high Omissions error rate.

All other behaviors noted as deviant through informal observation of this client were verified by the computer-based and other tests. Performance consistency over time was one of these. Here, Carl has developed a few self-help strategies and could apply these to boost accuracy during low cycles. For example, he applied "hyper-vigilance" for selected test items to score well for the short term; he also used a "chunking" technique that involves grouping similar words and/or letters for recall during the information processing tests. Yet, self-help strategies like these were inconsistent or totally omitted during longer tasks and the errors piled up.

Carl's overall profile therefore depicts the "spiky" performance style that typifies "limited alertness," the hallmark of a true Attention *Deficit* Disorder. He continued to lose focus periodically in distraction-free settings; and even simple tasks required much prompting and redirection under more stimulating conditions. Individuals like this cannot depend on themselves for precision, thus usually require and respond well to outside coaching and/or feedback from practice trials to fine-tune their actions. Unfortunately, life is fast-paced and unpredictable, thus may present insurmountable problems for one with inconsistent or random reactions in high stress situations.

## Trial and Outcome

I was called to testify regarding Carl's attention deficits in his penalty phase trial. Here, skillful questioning by the defense delineated both his strengths and weaknesses, with particular focus on the highly deviant scores he earned for three of the four variables of attention. The intention was to provide the jury with enough education regarding ADD/ADHD to assist them in determining an appropriate penalty. Coach A also testified, providing first-hand observations of the functional issues described above that extended my assessment results into everyday contexts.

In closing remarks, the defense reviewed Carl's ADD profile, linking it to his initial confusion captured on videotape as he entered the cluttered and highly stimulating store environment. His tendency to become overwhelmed in high stimulus test settings was used to explain Carl's attempt to steady himself by staring at the only uncluttered surfaces; namely, the counter and the back side of the cash register. This behavior was seen as an effort to "recover" cognitive focus by limiting visual distracters; but that didn't last long and, as the robbery commenced, continuing visual "overload" and the clerk's unpredictable actions lead to growing panic. Carl's inability to gain control under these conditions prompted his pleading demands of the noncompliant victim, as well as his final impulsive decision to shoot him. Indeed, distractibility throughout the disastrous incident had clouded any efforts at mature decision-making, resulting in a series of fast, bad decisions. Carl's final recorded statement appeared to rebuke the clerk for his "stupid" decision to defy orders: the body was found lying face up, more than ten feet away from the initial counter location.

In the final analysis, data derived from Carl's assessment helped to quantify that nebulous "something" described by the coach and to explain it to the penalty phase jury. Due to this and other advocacy on behalf of the client and his family, Carl was granted life without parole when the jury "hung" eight to four in opposing the death penalty.

## "Winning" LWOPP

Carl's case was successful from a trial attorney's perspective, in that he got Life Without the Possibility of Parole (LWOPP) in lieu of the death penalty. Although his grateful family cried tears of joy at this decision, it must be evaluated critically considering the probable outcomes for Carl and other "mildly" disabled inmates, such as George and Joseph, which are discussed below.

My first concern relates to the fact that treatment for ADD/ADHD is virtually nonexistent in California's correctional settings. Here, Ritalin, Cylert, and other such medications are restricted prescriptions which are not administered to inmates. I know of several cases where adult prisoners with attention disorders were drugged with antipsychotic medications to "calm" them, with disastrous effects. George is one such prisoner who was prescribed Lithium to ameliorate behaviors associated with his long term ADHD diagnosis. Unfortunately, corrections staff knew little about the potential side effects of this and other heat-sensitive medications until George suffered a seizure in the hot exercise yard. Since then, he has experienced intermittent seizures that require ongoing medical attention. You can learn more about George's ongoing struggles in Chapter Nineteen.

In California, Reception Centers that process incoming inmates assess certain skills related to academic and vocational ability via brief screening tests, but final placement decisions are far more concerned with an inmate's security rating due to past convictions, his commitment offense, and social affiliations (e.g., gang membership). As a result, Carl ended up in the maximum security housing unit (SHU) at California's notorious Pelican Bay facility. Placement there requires in-cell isolation for up to twenty-three hours per day, with one hour allotted for solitary recreation in an internal courtyard. Under these conditions, no educational, vocational, or other programming is accessible, regardless of disability verification in the Central file.

This is why Carl's court victory was anything but "winning" in a practical sense. His family now has to drive hundreds of miles for only the most minimal, infrequent visits with their increasingly disconnected son. In fact, many inmates housed in highly restricted SHU locations have developed severe psychoses from the relentless isolation. Accordingly, allegations of cruel and unusual punishment have been raised which are still being sorted out in civil courts.

Stories like Carl's may be what prompted Joseph, one of my earlier clients, to make what I saw as a strange request in light of the capital case against him. Here, we had just finished testing and he asked me whether my report might result in a life sentence instead of death. I was flummoxed at being asked this question, so I mumbled that it was possible and told him to confer with his attorney for more information. Joseph then said, "Do me a favor don't try too hard." He was, in essence, opting for death rather than the life Carl would now lead. We didn't listen, and he got a life sentence instead of the death penalty. The bottom line is that "winning" LWOPP is still losing, no matter how you look at it.

✧ ✧ ✧

I re-met Joseph almost ten years later while interviewing inmates at a central valley prison for the class action lawsuits described in Chapter Nineteen. He didn't seem to recognize me, nor I him. You see, over the years this formerly "buff" client had lost a lot of muscle tone and was missing several teeth from a fight that had broken out in the infamous SHU exercise pen. After a reminder, he recalled our assessment, mostly because the test rooms were in use that day, so it had taken place in the barber shop where he was strapped to a five-hundred pound chair. I then asked him about his "don't try too hard" request and how he felt about that today. To my relief, he said, "That was a punk kid talking. Nobody wants to die."

So, I guess it's fair to surmise that a life in prison is better than no life at all. Inmates carve out their own roles there, and adjust to the routine over time. I only hope that Carl has found some sort of purpose, perhaps through writing or meditation, in his sadly isolated existence.

* The Test of Variables of Attention (TOVA) is published by the TOVA Company, Freeland, Washington.

# CHAPTER FOUR
## Danny, ADHD and a Loaded Gun

This is the one case that *still* keeps me up at night. Whenever this happens, a number of variables swim around in my head: Danny's young age, the disability information that was omitted at his original trial, and the terrible outcome of the appeal trial two years later. This is his story.

### Background

Let's call this fourteen-year-old boy "Danny." He was the only son of a divorce situation where both parents had remarried and now had other kids. He now found himself shoved into a sort of "in-between" as a throwback reminder of an ancient failed relationship. The boy had lived with his mother in the years since the divorce, but had become a bit of a handful. This was partially due to internalized anger about his increasingly dissolving family ties, but it was mainly the result of his changing ADD condition.

Indeed, Attention Deficit Disorder, with or without Hyperactivity (ADHD), can be frustrating, especially as the child in question enters adolescence. This is because the medications that were successful a few years earlier may morph a bit with puberty. Some kids deviate so far as to have a weaker or even *opposite* reaction, thus titration under medical supervision is warranted. Some doctors recommend "going off medication" fully or just weekends, believing they are doing teenagers a favor by forcing them to "take charge" of their own behavior. Other kids refuse to take their meds at school due to embarrassment at having to leave the classroom for the daily trudge to the nurse's office. Whatever the case, the early teen years can be problematic for families of kids with ADD/ADHD.

When Danny started to exhibit bouts of fairly typical teenage volatility, his mother threw up her hands and sent him to live with his father in a strange town with entirely new family dynamics. I should note that, up until then, the youngster had continued his ADD medication with good results in terms of assisting self-control, and that the volatility that prompted his relocation happened when he was having an off-meds weekend. That's why it was unfortunate that, in the new living situation, Danny's ADD prescription was reportedly allowed to lapse.

Now school had just begun, and Danny entered ninth grade as the "new kid" in town, with limited self-controls and a lot of built-up anger. He had only been enrolled a week when the first disciplinary issue arose, and he was sent to the school office. A phone call to his stepmother aggravated the situation for a youngster who already believed he was on shaky ground. Now he faced threats of "grounding," corporal punishment, and possible eviction, with no allies but a pair of aging grandparents who lived out of state.

A week later, a second behavioral incident occurred, and Danny was sent home early on a one-day school suspension. He arrived at the house well before his nine-year-old half-sister and went to his room. Worried about the flak he would get when his working parents returned, Danny wandered around the house looking for a solution.

## The Crime and Arrest Interview

Okay, this is what I *think* happened from interviewing the attorneys and reviewing all available materials in this case: Danny found the gun in a storage closet and took it to his room. He was seriously contemplating suicide. Whether the gun was already loaded became a debatable, but critical, factor as the case unfolded. All I know for sure is that, playing around with the gun, Danny shot through his mattress into the floor (fact). A second random misfire resulted in a hole through his window screen, with the bullet landing somewhere in the adjacent woods. A short time later, the youth heard his half-sister come home and hid the gun under the covers of his unmade bed. She entered his room and sat down on the floor with her back against the bed and proceeded to chat about her day at school. Do I have to tell you the rest? Picture the trigger of a loaded gun covered by only a bed sheet and projecting menacingly near restless fingers and toes. Throw in antsiness and wiggling in the now unmedicated boy, just the right angle between the gun barrel and his sister's head ...

It all adds up to my Personal Mantra #1: Untreated ADD + Gun = Disaster.

The disorganized state of Danny's mind over the next twenty-four hours was clearly depicted in the videotaped police interview that followed. Here, the kindly male police officer patiently pries the story out, arm around the boy's shaking shoulders. At first, Danny can't recall much of anything and can offer no precise details of events (only that something *really bad* happened), so the officer "assists" by prodding certain leading words with logistical questions. The officer's skillful techniques work and, little by little, the truth comes out. How had something bad happened to his sister? Who was sitting where? How had she ended up bleeding in an empty bathtub? What did Danny mean when he said he had to "clean up something," down the hallway but couldn't recall what?

Why did he go into the woods to think things over, and how had he fallen asleep? Why didn't he return home until the next day, and what did he think had happened when he saw all the police cars? As the officer pries the last little memory free, Danny breaks down in sobs: He remembers it all.

I want to stress here that the interviewing police officer was made aware of Danny's ADHD condition, but took no action to call an appropriate advocate for the youth. What he did instead was to offer friendship and understanding *("You're the only boy, huh? ... That's got to be kind of tough")* so as to gain enough trust to proceed. He then very methodically broke the kid down so as to obtain a confession. In the final analysis, regardless of the officer's training and dedication to duty, it seems highly unethical to interview a distraught fourteen-year-old with a known history of attention deficits, without an advocate present to facilitate and monitor accurate two-way communication. According to Danny's defense team, the interview took place without the presence of legal counsel because neither of Danny's parents came forward to insist that one be present.

## The Trial

Killing your sister at age fourteen in Danny's conservative state entitles you to trial as an adult. I might note that fifteen additional states allow fourteen-year-olds to be tried as adults, while three others have reduced the age to twelve, and at least seventeen states have *no minimum age* at all. In Danny's case, defense attorneys appear to have been stymied in any attempt to explain ADD and the unformed teenaged brain. As a result they were completely unable to offer a viable explanation as to how this accidental shooting could have occurred. They wouldn't listen to Danny's only allies, his grandparents, who begged them to look into his ADD. Instead, they put on a mechanical and unconvincing defense, hoping to play on the sympathies of juror parents with kids about Danny's age.

Conversely, the prosecution laid out a strong case, depicting the boy as a plotting, angry kid who acted maliciously out of jealousy toward his half-sister. They then called Danny's father to the witness stand in order to further support this argument. You see, in this state it was, and probably still is, illegal to leave a loaded gun in any unlocked storage space that is accessible to minor children. Hence, the father's testimony that the gun was previously *unloaded* suggested that the boy *must have loaded it himself*. This nicely backed up the prosecution's claim of premeditated murder versus a tragic and bumbling accident. Accordingly, Danny was found guilty and sent to an *adult prison* for a long term of confinement.

## Appeal

This case was taken up on appeal when Danny's grieving and relentless grandparents discovered some sort of jury impropriety at his original trial. By now, the boy had suffered two long years of daily torture as a juvenile living inside an adult prison. In this regard, I would refer the reader to research, covered briefly in Chapter Eighteen, that documents their immediate and persistent sexual abuse by adult inmates. This and other age-based mistreatment correlates with and explains the high rate of suicides by juveniles placed in these facilities. If there were *ever* grounds for alleging "cruel and unusual punishment," the plight of juveniles in adult prisons would serve as the ultimate example.

Danny's grandparents were successful in their fight for a new trial and hired an appellate defense team to proceed with the case. These lawyers had apparently heard about my work with cognitive disabilities from colleagues in another state and called for a consultation. Since the court would not award funding to fly me to Danny's location for an actual assessment, I was asked to submit a sort of position paper which could help describe ADD and its effects on adolescent development. From the rather comprehensive materials I was given—school and medical records, the arrest videotape, grandparent affidavits, trial transcripts, and so forth—I could make a pretty good case explaining the behavioral effects of this youth's ADD on and off medication. I was then able to link his off-meds functioning to the bumbling accident itself, as well as his failed recall of events and personal disorganization immediately following the shooting.

After reviewing my report, Danny's defense team requested that I appear in court to testify; but, again, the court (the *same* court which was responsible for incarcerating a child with adults in the first place) refused funding. I was so far into the case by now that I made them an offer: I was coming east to see family in two months on my own dime and would testify, pro bono, if the court would only grant this small time extension. To my undying horror, the answer was *NO*. The defense was hogtied and again lost the case. Sixteen-year-old Danny was returned to the same adult prison.

I rarely take cases to heart—it's more professional, and better for me personally, to remain uninvolved. But this one still haunts me when I think of Danny's cruel fate. I can only hope his small support system continues to press for parole when it becomes available. But, in the long run, this is a case where the damage, now extensive, is done and baked into the cake. Not one, but two, young lives were snuffed out in a fatal accident that was horrible, stupid, and preventable. Had Danny's difficult transition been assisted with better medical, home, and school support, perhaps this story would have had a different ending.

# CHAPTER FIVE
## John, Bungled Copy-Cat Burglary

In the Preface to this book I described how, following the successful conclusion of that first case (Omar), news of my involvement traveled through the public defense community. Two weeks later my phone rang and a charismatic Public Defender named Andy convinced me to take on his death penalty case.

Andy accompanied me to my first meeting with his client, which took place inside the Attorney Room of the Men's Central Jail in downtown Los Angeles. I remember little about this meeting other than my fear of being locked inside the jail's double security doors should an earthquake disrupt electrical power. That's the comforting thing about older jails and prisons—they still use actual *keys* to get you in and out.

So, this is how I first met John, a twenty-six-year-old African-American man who had committed murder in the course of a home invasion robbery. He was known to have Specific Learning Disabilities that affected reading and spelling, and therefore required a comprehensive assessment of these and other academic skills. But his most salient difficulties, even in casual interactions, involved expressive and receptive spoken language which made ordinary conversation challenging, both for John and his listener. Andy had detected John's language immaturity in their earliest meetings and had been searching for someone who could explain it to a penalty phase jury, if necessary. It looked like I got the job.

## Language-Based Learning Disabilities

Much has been written about language processing differences in Learning Disabled students and defendants. Many of these individuals are found to be deficient in the use of *internal language*, the "private speech" needed to mediate one's own actions. This deficiency can affect personal organization and self control, both of which have been linked to criminal behavior. Over several decades of testing, I have found it typical for individuals with language-based Learning Disabilities to employ ineffective nonverbal imagery to make initial choices, as well as to modify adaptive decisions once an action is underway. Processing information in this less mature, sometimes random manner greatly increases the likelihood of errors of *omission*, where not all information is received, and *commission*, where inaccurate information can result in behavioral confusion. Let me provide an example of the sort of nonverbal processing which I came across repeatedly in testing these individuals.

One of the information processing tests I employed required the subject to view lengthening chains of pictured items for immediate recall. The most effective recall strategy for this task involves using internal language to label and order the items. Mature thinkers do this automatically, using a technique known as "verbal rehearsal." Repeating the item names to themselves in this way, adults can typically recall seven (plus or minus two) items, usually in the order presented. When clients recalled far fewer items or provided them in random order, I knew immediately they were not using internal language to master the task. Asked, "How are you remembering these items?" one Learning Disabled (LD) test subject said he was "just looking at them and thinking." This method, if you can call it that, is something we might expect to see in far younger children, but not in subjects with adult language competence.

Language immaturity also affects one's ability to organize and monitor input on a continuing basis. This is why LD students often appear disorganized, relying instead on impulse, guesswork, and luck. A person like this tends to undertake new activities armed with what I call "half-plans"; that is, poorly thought-out images of desired outcomes, that fail to conceptualize the small steps needed to actually reach their goals. Then, when things fall apart, the individual does not have sufficient internal language to correct his defective plan through self-coaching. People who do not routinely think through possible consequences of their actions are more likely to act first, then encounter and deal with the fallout later. This typical LD behavior has been described in a wonderful PBS training video* as: ***"Ready ... Fire ... Aim!"***

Internal language (also known as "private speech" or self-talk) is therefore a necessary ingredient for generating and maintaining self-control in any complex, stressful, or escalating situation. That's why special educators directly teach learning and language disabled students ways they can employ self-talk to curb random impulses and effect more positive outcomes. Some teachers coach students to Stop, Think, Act, and Review their own actions. A similar approach directs them to ask the following self-questions both initially, and as tasks get underway: *What is my problem? What is my plan? Am I using my plan? How is it working?* The bottom line is that internal language does not typically guide individuals with language-based Learning Disabilities. Instead, they appear to make initial decisions and mid-task adaptations in random fashion, and are typically quite surprised when things go wrong.

## John's "Plan"

Hanging around his apartment complex with nothing much to do, John hatched a "plan" based on a similar one that had been successful for an acquaintance. The idea here was to visit neighboring apartments pretending to be some sort of tenant advocate collecting information about needed repairs. The successful acquaintance had carried a notebook in which he jotted down complaints of broken windows and doors, leaky faucets, and the like. He also collected information as to the various tenants' work schedules under the pretense of needing it to make repair appointments. This made it easy to return to a specific apartment when the tenant was out and burglarize the place, taking valuable items he had scoped out on the initial visit.

John very much liked his friend's master plan and decided to copy it at his own apartment complex. He began by buying a pen and small notebook, but that was apparently the extent of his pre-planning effort. Notations in the notebook indicate that he visited three apartments around dinner time one Friday evening. At the first of these, apartment #202, no one was home so he moved on to #203. The tenant he spoke with there made several complaints which John attempted to write down in his notebook. This explained the notation, "203 door back one," as well as other more mysterious notations and misspellings. This information was apparently filed away for a later burglary as planned.

Now he rang the bell at apartment #204 which was answered by a middle-aged woman with a paring knife in her hand. She explained in broken English that she was cooking dinner and invited John inside to talk while the last vegetables were prepared. It was then that John apparently lost track of his "plan," abandoning it in favor of a full-on robbery. He drew a gun and told the woman to hand over all her money. She rummaged through her purse but found little, so she offered to write John a check.

He accepted it.

It was at this point that John forced the woman into her bedroom. Why he did so remains unclear, but it appears to have been an attempt to look for jewelry or other valuable items.

Unfortunately, the woman misunderstood (or maybe not), believing his intention was to rape her. She started to undress but suddenly panicked and began screaming. Having lost all control of the situation at that point, John picked up the paring knife she had left on the dresser and stabbed her shoulder "a little bit" in order to "quiet her down" (quotes are John's). To his surprise, this proved ineffective, and the woman instead tried to run from the bedroom. That was when John shot and killed her. Before leaving, he stuffed a couple of items from her jewelry box into his pocket.

John was arrested at the bank the following Monday morning trying to cash his victim's check. A gold chain belonging to her was still in his pocket. A most interesting police interrogation of this language disabled man followed.

### Interrogation

In Chapter One, I gave an example of a typical method employed by police officers to question criminal suspects. It teams up two officers, one "friendly," the other adversarial, who take turns questioning the defendant until a confession is obtained. While the "bad cop" bullies and scares the suspect, his partner offers friendly alternatives that will help him "later on in court." Many times, false evidence is dangled during an interrogation, including one truly outrageous (cartooned) situation where fake "lie detector" results were introduced. Here, officers placed the hapless suspect next to an ordinary copy machine and taped a couple of miscellaneous wires to his head, with the other ends thrown behind the copier. They then placed a paper that said "LIE" in bold letters face down inside the copier lid. Every time the suspect attempted to defend himself, they pushed the "print" button and confronted him with the undeniable proof that he was, "lying again"!

The interrogation technique used in John's case resulted in an amazing array of six different stories as he tried to wiggle out of arrest. As expected, Story #1 was something like, "I don't even know that lady." When it was pointed out that he had left his notebook inside her apartment, John modified Story #2 somewhat: he was having an illicit affair with her and simply left something behind. At this point, the "bad cop" apparently realized they had a suspect with childlike capabilities on their hands. He therefore employed a strategy that never failed to extract more from the defendant, namely, they threatened to leave John all alone in the interrogation room. This, along with a reminder that he was arrested trying to cash her check at the bank, prompted Story #3, that John and the woman were "running drugs" together and this was his payment.

As the officers kept threatening to leave the room, John concocted two more explanations before folding completely. One of these (Story #4) was that he saw the probable killer, an unidentified Asian man, run out the woman's back door and could now help the officers find him ("Let's get him!") Another threat by the officers to walk out and leave him alone led to Story #5, which was even worse than what had really happened: John claimed to be a "hit man" who was simply following instructions to kill her. The officers' final threat resulted in Story #6, his actual confession. To John's sad surprise, opting to finally "tell his side of the story" did not secure the help officers typically promise, either immediately (no Diet Coke) or later on in court.

John's interrogation performance is entirely consistent with the sort of juvenile thinking associated with many other cognitive disorders described in this book. In this sense, he demonstrates no "presupposition," a term used by language specialists to describe one's ability to make logical assumptions. In other words, a mature thinker in John's shoes would realize that 1) the officers already know of his involvement and probable guilt, 2) they have several items of proof in their possession, and 3) his stories are entirely unrealistic and hence not believable. Instead, John offers story after story, childishly believing that they will buy one of them and let him go.

## Specific Language Issues at Interrogation

Certain interesting verbal exchanges between John and the officers clearly demonstrated bi-directional communication issues. In some of these, the language disabled client joined a host of others (See Appendix B) who had trouble understanding the particular language of questions posed by the officers. One such exchange concerned the fact that John's sister and her boyfriend saw him enter their apartment in a big hurry just after the murder was thought to have occurred.

| | |
|---|---|
| Officer: | Both your sister and Mike said you came home ... |
| John: | Both my sisters? No. One of my sisters was at work. |
| Officer: | Huh? No, I said both your sister and Mike said ... |
| John: | There you go saying both my sisters again. One of 'em was at work. |
| Officer: | Wait a minute, wait a minute! Both your sister (holding up one finger) and Mike (holding up a second finger)—see, there's *two* of them—they <u>both</u> said ... |
| John: | Oh. |

Here, you can see the client's initial confusion, the officer's eventual and very effective accommodation, and John's final reception of content. The penny drops—he understands ("Oh").

Examples of expressive language failure were numerous throughout the interview. Here's but one exchange where John can't come up with an individual word so the officer provides it for him.

| | |
|---|---|
| Officer: | Where did he go? |
| John: | He ran by ... uh ... Got this big old thing in back ... the ... the ... |
| Officer: | The *planter* in the back? |
| John: | Yeah, there you go. |

In a second exchange we can see just how much external assistance John needs to express a complete thought. Here, he is trying to explain how the unidentified Asian perpetrator left the victim's apartment, and he's having a heck of a time doing it.

| | |
|---|---|
| John: | He ran down ... |
| Officer: | He ran down where? |
| John: | He ran ... he ... |
| Officer: | He ran *down the stairs?* |
| John: | ... ran down the stairs. |
| Officer: | And you *followed him down the stairs*. |
| John: | ... followed him down the stairs. |

A review of the arrest transcript verifies that, as John became increasingly overwhelmed, officers stepped in to provide words and phrases that he simply parroted back. This occurred frequently enough that one might question just <u>who</u> was providing the factual information in the case. Indeed, John's performance throughout the interview raised great concerns considering that a suspect's transcribed admissions can, and usually will, be used to convict him in court. In the end, it was John's Story #6 confession that led the State to seek the death penalty against him.

**Trial and Outcome**

Since this was my first trial testimony, I would have been nervous anyway; but my anxiety was exacerbated by the fact that I was the *only* witness for the defense, and a man's life was hanging in the balance. Contrary to what is typically shown on TV, the courtroom was empty of spectators with the exception of the family of the murder victim. They were seated just behind the prosecutor who made sure to place the podium so that I could see them. They looked like nice people, and I felt sympathy for them, but I had a job to do. The judge was a woman who had tried to make the courtroom somewhat "homey" by hanging a few pictures on the walls. Despite this, and a pleasant looking jury, approaching the witness stand felt like a march to my own execution.

The prosecutor in John's case was a zealous Assistant District Attorney (ADA) who was well known in the local defense community. It was rumored that a dart board hanging on his office wall had John's picture in the center. Other gossip described him as having a belt with notches carved in the leather for each death verdict. I have no idea whether any of this was true, but can verify that his demeanor at trial was rough and intimidating. But John's defense attorney had two good things going for him in presenting the penalty phase of this case. First, the presiding judge apparently had prior experience with the disagreeable prosecutor and dealt with him sternly whenever he was out of line. She also recognized the defense's "star witness" (me) as a first timer on the stand who was scared to the point of nausea. She therefore informed the ADA in a side bar that I was a "nice lady," and that he should watch his step. If what followed was his idea of going easy, I would hate to be exposed to a full-on attack.

My examination by the defense focused on presenting John's learning and language disabilities in logical fashion. Attorney Andy was assisted here by the judge's fairly consistent decisions to overrule the ADA's petulant objections to virtually everything he could. I was therefore able to present a fairly comprehensive picture of John in childhood, and currently, as an adult with language-based Learning Disabilities.

It was now the ADA's turn to try and impeach my previous testimony. He couldn't. When he made no headway in assaulting my credentials, John's historical diagnosis, or the current test results, he produced a Xeroxed school transcript and plopped it on the witness stand. This document listed several passing grades John had earned in high school, including one for Driver's Ed. He then asked me to look at the top of the page and read the printed header aloud. I couldn't see anything there and stated so. The ADA's annoyance was quite obvious as he repeated the request, adding that it was "plain to see" so as to make me look like an idiot. When I again responded that I couldn't find any text, he asked to approach the stand and snatched up the paper. *Surprise!* The header he referred to had been Xeroxed off my copy. The ADA grumbled this finding to the court, crumpled the page into a ball, and tossed it free-throw style toward the Court Clerk's wastepaper basket. He missed the shot and lost the jury. Oh, and that passing grade for Driver's Ed? Very nice, but John's actual driver's license listed the gender as "F" due to his error in completing the application.

It's not every day that the defense is assisted by such unappealing opposing counsel at trial, or for judges to rule against one side in such a consistent manner. Maybe the obnoxious ADA just deserved it, I wouldn't really know. Whatever the case, the jury negated the death penalty in favor of a life sentence for John. The ADA would have one less notch to carve on his belt this time.

* The video mentioned above is entitled "Understanding Learning Disabilities: How Difficult Can This Be?" PBS Video, 1989.

# CHAPTER SIX
# Gil, Bragging to Impress

Whenever I think of Gil, the phrase, "third time's a charm" comes to mind. That's how many court trials it took to conclude a shocking thing that I suspected right from the start: Gil was completely innocent! And I haven't said that more than twice in all the years I conducted these assessments. It wasn't my job to make this sort of determination, but merely to assess a referred individual and hand the results over to the people tasked with the ultimate decision.

The overweight twenty-five-year-old Hispanic man who sat before me had no history of special education. Nevertheless, there was a certain *something* discerned by his lawyer, who had worked with me on several previous cases, that required further assessment. Attorney Jonathan therefore contacted me with a request to examine all of his immature client's behaviors and skills, because he had a sense something was wrong. This is Gil's story.

## Assessment

I'll begin with Gil's assessment because it will lay the proper foundation to discuss how easily he was lured to confess to a murder he didn't commit. I could see right away that Jonathan was right—something was "off" about his client, and it was now time to find out what it was. I had arranged his test session at a newer jail in the north part of Los Angeles County. It was a long drive, but well worth it because of its friendly and accommodating visitation staff and the large private rooms they made available for assessment. I settled in for the long day that was usually required to examine a person's skills across the board.

In that no background documents related to Gil's schooling were available, I was forced to obtain a brief history from the client himself. This can be a bit tricky, in that people usually only tell you what they want you to know. However, pressing the client with a few follow-up questions yielded an acceptable version of the truth. He reported attending a public elementary school with "good" grades and attendance, then moving on to a junior high which was also in his neighborhood. Gil noted that he "skipped" the latter half of seventh grade to enter eighth grade early. Pressed as to why such a thing had been done, he finally admitted it was an attempt to close the age gap created by one or more grade retentions in elementary school. So, his previous self-report of academic success was clearly a cover for some degree of early school failure. Consequently it was not surprising that, after three years of high school, the youth dropped out to enter the world of work. Assisted by an acquaintance, he was successful in landing a job as a night shift security guard for a local business.

My subsequent assessment of Gil found a severe discrepancy between his verbal (72) and nonverbal (96) IQ scores. The twenty-four point gap between these two subskills comes close to that needed to diagnose "*aphasia*," a brain-based language disorder, thus a speech and language evaluation was recommended. This particular test finding, along with Standard Scores that bottomed off tests of vocabulary (51) and language fundamentals (63), described a person who relied on his better nonverbal skills (looking and doing) to compensate for a *severe* verbal discrepancy. Additional tests showed sixth grade reading and math skills which did not qualify as formal Learning Disabilities via the current educational description; nevertheless, Gil's severely discrepant verbal, and very weak auditory processing skills, did reach this level of severity.

To give you an idea of just how discrepant some of these skills were, think of a five-to-eight-year-old child trying to encode high level language and abstract concepts, and then respond with answers intended to please his conversational partner. That's exactly what Gil did that landed him in the current legal predicament. To make matters even worse, he did so under the charged emotional conditions of a gang-style threat.

### Case Investigation

A fatal drive-by shooting had occurred in an East Los Angeles neighborhood where two local gangs were constantly at war with each other. It seemed rather apparent that the shooter almost had to be a member of Gang A, which meant he would have been at war with the members of Gang B. On the night in question, the Gang B member was shot and killed outside his home by a bullet that neighbors described as coming from a passing car. Police began interviewing members of Gang A but were getting nowhere using the standard tactic off hauling suspects into the station to be interviewed. That's when they brought in a young, female detective to collect undercover information while posing as a "home girl" from Gang A's self-proclaimed neighborhood.

I'm not sure how or when "Gracie" first met Gil in person, but she did a good job of luring him into the suspect net via several subsequent telephone contacts. These calls were transcribed and provided to the defense prior to introducing them in court. One of the conversations began with Gil describing a favor for a female friend which involved watching over her home while she vacationed in Mexico. He tells Gracie that his friend's father brings prostitutes there whenever she goes away, so it's his job to roust them out. Gracie feigns respect for his loyalty and prowess, asking what he would do if he encountered prostitutes at the house. Gil's bragging answer ("I'd kick them out. I'd be like, eh, they got to get out. This is my home girl's house") was clearly provided to impress the attractive detective. She later asks, "So, I'm your home girl too, right?" Gil agrees, "Yeah, you're number one," and the undercover interrogation continues.

Gracie refocuses what was becoming a rambling and pointless conversation to ask Gil the names of his friends and whether they are all members of Gang A. This is where Gil attempts to act tough by asserting his "moniker" and vaguely alleging Gang A affiliation. The pretense continues until the undercover officer asks if he ever takes drugs, and Gil emphatically denies it ("Oh, nah, nah—never—nah, nah, nah.") In fact, he had good reason to avoid recreational drugs, in that his security guard job required periodic urine samples to insure sobriety. However, his (probably truthful) denial changed substantially when Gracie shared that she had "tried it a couple times." After his initial surprise ("Oh, you tried it?"), Gil then attempts to impress her by answering, "Yeah, I tried the coke through your nose, but that's about it." He ends by fabricating an impression that he would actually rather *sell* than *use* drugs because, "You can't do 'em both."

In the next transcribed phone call, Gracie returns to the line of questioning intended to verify Gil's association with "gangbangers." He begins by again denying it, saying that people just spread "stupid rumors if you do ... Like if somebody's got shot or something, they'd be like, oh, it was them." To keep Gil talking, Gracie flatters him saying, "Dang, Dude, you got some exciting stories." This pretty much cinches it: if Gil doesn't have anything "exciting" to convey, he will almost certainly make something up to continue impressing her. Before too long he's bragging about shooting at people but missing them due to his "bad aim" at night.

## The Sting

All of the above was enough to raise questions as to whether Gil may have been the shooter in the Gang B murder, so the local police arranged another undercover contact. I'll refer to this person as "O.G." because he was, indeed, an Old Gang member from Gil's neighborhood who had been in and out of prison for years. O.G. was well known in the local gang culture as someone with street credibility who was backed up by a network of tough, vicious gangsters. As such, he was someone to be feared.

Gil was at home one afternoon when O.G., wired by police to record the conversation, appeared at the door wanting to talk with him about the shooting. Mixed into a huge amount of peripheral conversation, O.G. issued a serious threat that centered around a potential "green light" if Gil didn't admit his role in the shooting. Confused? Well, anyone trying to read the transcribed conversation between these two "homies" would be. The term "green light" refers to a gang-style hit on a targeted person. O.G. was telling Gil that his life was in danger unless he confessed to the drive-by shooting immediately. Somehow, his admission would be relayed by O.G. to the powers that be, and the green light would be cancelled. Or something.

The point is that Gil was coerced into agreeing to a murder he not only didn't commit, but couldn't accurately describe. Here, credible sources had reported the shooting as a "drive-by," but Gil described it quite differently, saying that he, "parked the truck in the driveway ... and walked out, and I walked out, you know, I walked up." When O.G. responds with praise ("That's right. That's right. You did right ..."), Gil is emboldened to continue his fabricated story, stating, "But it was no drive-by, you know, because I didn't want to shoot ... no families, no guys, nothing, only gangbangers you know, 'cause we're gangbanging." Their continuing discussion revealed that he didn't even know the precise kind of gun that was involved. Gil therefore throws in a few swear words and street terms to emphasize how tough he is. Now that the lie is out there, he seems unable to stop relating the fantasized scenario to O.G. These repetitious statements suggest he was merely trolling for additional praise.

Gil was soon arrested and charged with the drive-by murder. It was, however, his lucky day when Jonathan was appointed as his lawyer. That's because this seasoned attorney spared no amount of effort or expense in hiring a former police officer with expertise in interrogation and confessions, along with me to conduct the assessment described above. All of us agreed that Gil was undoubtedly innocent of the murder, but tricked into exaggerating a gang affiliation by a cute female investigator, and then coerced into a confession by a scary gang member used as bait by the local police. Clearly, the term "green light" was purposely inserted in the conversation by O.G. because it elicits a high level of fear in neighborhoods where the gang culture flourishes. The entire exchange between Gil and O.G. thus amounted to little more than a coerced confession which Jonathan would later attempt to suppress at trial.

**Trial(s)**

Three court trials in different locations followed, each of which resulted in a "hung" jury. Jonathan met with me, along with his investigator and a paralegal, to brainstorm the best strategy to present Gil's learning and language deficits to the jury. My test findings would serve as a foundation to then present the investigator's testimony regarding the serious ethical breeches that surrounded the two undercover interviews. Investigator "Dan," a former police officer, had many years of experience using various interrogation methods to interview crime suspects. He was also a stickler for following departmental rules regarding suspect interviews.

Strict adherence to these policies had two purposes: First, providing standard due process to the suspect would insure that any information revealed during a subsequent interview would not be thrown out in court; but more important (to me), using the proper arrest protocol helped to insure *fundamental fairness* to suspects with cognitive limitations like Gil's. I will tell you that Dan was absolutely livid regarding what he considered to be underhanded tactics involving the use of both undercover individuals. One had been used to lure Gil in, and the other to deliver the knock-down punch in the form of a coercive threat. Jonathan's motion to suppress both interviews was based on these facts, plus my assessment that verified his client's cognitive immaturity. Most of it was, nevertheless, allowed in at trial.

### Outcome(s)

Having to testify once in a murder case is stressful enough, but to repeat it twice more is daunting, especially before such varied juries. The first of these was composed of working class people who looked attentive as we laid out the role Gil's learning and language disabilities had played in his entrapment by the local police. This jury nevertheless came back seven to five in favor of guilt. Accordingly, Jonathan reconvened the troops to face a second jury in a more upscale neighborhood which was stocked with well educated people. In fact, it would not be going too far to state that Jury #2 contained one or more "rocket scientists" who worked at a famous laboratory in a Los Angeles suburb. Many of these jurors took notes as they conscientiously listened to all of the evidence.

This time, Jonathan and I focused more pointedly on the undercover gang member's recognition of Gil's language deficits and his efforts to use them in securing a false confession. To do this, we presented ways that even untrained speakers adjust their verbal utterances to accommodate people they perceive as less than competent listeners. We cited four such accommodations used repeatedly by O.G. which included: speaking in reduced terms, checking for ongoing understanding, asking Gil to better explain his responses, and checking to be sure he received the full intent of the threatening message. These and similar adjustments (some of which are footnoted at the end of this chapter) were rampant throughout the conversation that unfolded. The jury apparently understood these issues and our related arguments fairly well, because they came back eleven to one in favor of a Not Guilty verdict. In fact, complaints were made by several jurors who described the single hold-out as an attention seeking "troublemaker." Let me add here that most jurors who find themselves the only one opposing a Not Guilty verdict will capitulate to the others; whereas, a single hold-out for *innocence* will often maintain his position, because incarcerating an innocent person is a far greater injustice than the reverse situation. That's why the single hold-out for Guilt on Jury #2 was disconcerting, and doubly so, because a unanimous decision would have ended the whole ordeal.

The second hung jury meant doing it all over again, this time back in a working class neighborhood adjacent to the one where the first trial was held. Dan and I repeated our testimonies, this time with a different prosecutor, a woman in her early forties who worked hard to insure that the shady interviews were heard as acceptable ways to conduct police business. Once again the jury retired for deliberation and took some time before coming back with their deadlocked verdict: seven to five, Not Guilty. Whether the state would seek a fourth trial was up to the D.A. who now walked out of the courtroom with an annoyed look on her face. After a few weeks without a filing, Jonathan called to say that the charges had finally been dropped. Gil was released from jail more than three years after his initial arrest.

Did Gil learn a lesson here? I certainly hope so. No more bragging about being a "gangbanger" to impress people. No more falling for sham flattery or threats. Indeed, a smarter, more street savvy twenty-eight-year-old left custody that week, hopefully, never to return.

## More About the Transcribed Interview Comments

In the first ten pages of the coerced O.G. interview, the older gang member checked to insure Gil's understanding thirty-five times over eighty-two utterances, repeatedly using comments like, "You know what I mean?" and "See what I'm saying?" Conversely, Gil responds with confusion, saying, "What?" or "What happened?" more than a dozen times, and provides thirty-seven separate comments of "Yeah" as he struggles to process and absorb OG's threatening verbal content. What follows is an example of the discussion between the two conversational partners that sets the stage for Gil's later arrest.

| | |
|---|---|
| O.G: | Okay, so see, 'cause they're, like I said, they're saying it's a drive-by. [NOTE: That's because it WAS a drive-by shooting.] |
| Gil: | It wasn't no drive-by man, it was, I was right there. |
| O.G: | So, you got out the truck. |
| Gil: | Yeah, I got out the truck. |
| O.G: | And they, so, they didn't see the (gun) out? |
| Gil: | What happened? |
| O.G: | They didn't see? |
| Gil: | Nah, they didn't see it man, 'cause, pack up something, like, you know, like (gun). You know, so, whatever, you know. |
| O.G: | Okay, okay, so you (shot)? |
| Gil: | Yeah me and (friend's name), yeah, we (shot). |
| O.G: | You guys both (shot)? [NOTE: Evidence showed there was only one shooter.] |
| Gil: | Nah, me and him, you know? Well I was ... 'cause he couldn't handle it, you know, 'cause (the gun) was a little one—it was a big one. |
| O.G: | Yeah, I know what it was. |

Gil: Yeah, it was ...
O.G: It was a rifle.
Gil: Yeah, yeah, something like that.
O.G: Believe me, dog.
Gil: But it was some like a machine gun or something like that ... but it was, like, a rifle. [NOTE: Well, which was it? Ballistic evidence suggests this is not a debatable question.]
O.G: Okay. Who'd you guys get the (gun) from?
Gil: What happened?
O.G: Who'd you get it from?
Gil: He bought it.
O.G: Okay, okay, so yeah, you know what I'm saying?
Gil: Yeah, 'cause whatever, you know.

With conversational skills this weak, it's remarkable that <u>any</u> information was obtained at all. O.G. really had his work cut out for him, in that Gil required *much* prompting and repetition to even begin to understand the proposed "hit" he now faced. Then, once the penny dropped, he made up a false account and continued to spew it out for another several pages of the transcript. As Jonathan's investigator told the judge, if an interviewer can break enough rules and pose a severe enough threat, he can get <u>anyone</u> to admit to something he didn't do. Even the judge.

# CHAPTER SEVEN
# Lenny, Mock Jury Trial

I had an interesting death penalty appeal case out of Chicago a few years after I established my private practice. The client, Lenny, had been on Death Row for twenty years for the accidental shooting of a bank security guard during a three-person robbery. Lenny suffered from multiple disabilities including speech and hearing issues, learning disabilities, a psychiatric disorder, and neurological damage; yet, none of these factors were made known to the jury during the original trial. This was now the job of the very capable Appellate Division in the Illinois Public Defender's (PD) Office, which hired four experts, one for each disability area, to assist in overturning the death verdict. I was the one asked to test Lenny for ongoing Learning Disabilities, and did so at the Chicago jail where he had been transferred pending the appeal.

### Status of the Case

In Illinois, all capital (death penalty) cases actually require two verdicts. The first of these merely qualifies the defendant as death penalty *eligible*; the second decides whether he should, indeed, be *executed*. Juries in these cases must answer both questions in a two-step trial process. The State PD had secured approval to retry Lenny's penalty phase case before a new jury in the Chicago court system. This meant presenting the case all over again, but this time, with the addition of four experts who would testify as to the client's disabilities.

## Assessment Meeting

No jail or prison I ever visited had the unusual entry gizmo used in Chicago's Cook County Jail. Here, all visitors had to enter through a high tech "booth" before proceeding into the housing units. The booth was actually a scanner of sorts where the visitor was instructed to stand for a few seconds while a puff of air shot up from the floor, passed over and through his or her clothing, and was sucked up into a reader in the top. Potential visitors then waited while the reader analyzed them for drugs and other contraband. Only when cleared via this analysis could the visitor enter the interior of the jail. I passed through the scanner several times to test clients in this jail and always found it both creative and delightful in a weird sort of way. Nevertheless, assuming the scanner is still in use and required for both professional and informal visitors, I recommend that ladies wear skirts made of heavy enough fabric to prevent a reenactment of Marilyn Monroe's "Bus Stop" scenario.

I met with Lenny in an interior interview room framed on three sides with large plate glass windows. Looking back now, I think the space may have had prior use as a control booth for deputies because two hallways were viewable from this corner location. As such, activity inside and outside the room was on full bidirectional view. Fearing this would be distracting to Lenny, I faced him toward the only solid wall in the room. That meant I was the one facing toward the windows and, yes, I will admit it was a bit distracting due to the considerable amount of activity taking place in the hallway. We settled in for the day with orders to have a lunch tray brought in for Lenny and bathroom breaks as needed. Due to the scanner gizmo, I hadn't even tried to sneak any food inside, electing instead to fast during the several hour process. This problem was alleviated somewhat when the trustee who delivered Lenny's lunch accessed an extra orange juice to help me get through the day.

I must say that Lenny was a pleasure to test and interact with. He was a favorite of guards at the prison that had been his twenty-year home because he literally "saved" one of them from an assault. This reputation had followed him to his current jail setting, where guards appeared to treat him with a certain amount of dignity and respect. Now forty-five years old, he had also developed a good deal of maturity over the years, and had connected with his God through the prison ministry. The result was a subject who was relaxed, amiable, and totally cooperative throughout the assessment. He knew what was on the line, but had come to terms with it long ago. His fears were even further alleviated when the governor of Illinois became the first in the nation to impose a moratorium on the death penalty.

## Assessment Findings

This client's binaural hearing problem had been medically linked to chronic sinusitis which was surgically treated on more than one occasion. Lenny described his current difficulties as "clogged" ears that "pop open" quite unexpectedly at times. The prison doctor had been made aware of this condition, and indicated to Lenny that it was "something to check out" at some point in the future. Being that he was on Death Row, I wondered when that might be. Most important to this discussion is the fact that Lenny's hearing defect had been documented since his earliest school days. In file comments, one teacher indicated the need to "shout" at him to gain his attention, and another one recommended training in lip-reading to assist communication. The present evaluation nevertheless noted adequate ability to receive instructions delivered at a moderate volume; but the fact that particular speech sounds such as *th*, *k*, and *br* were not fully articulated in Lenny's casual speech suggested ongoing problems with their reception.

As a youth, Lenny attended public schools in Chicago, where he was originally enrolled in the regular class program. Within a few weeks, it became apparent that he had difficulty following instructions and keeping up with classmates. This led to a series of referrals to various specialists whose tests yielded highly inconsistent results. For example, a 1961 (age six) psychological assessment reported a full scale IQ score of only 71; while subsequent evaluations yielded scores of 93 (1964) and 85 (1967). There are several things that could account for such variation—among them, emotional mood swings, ADD, escalating mental illness, examiner error, willful noncompliance and, of course, hearing loss caused by intermittent blockage in the inner ear. Since all of these scores were obtained thirty-five to forty years earlier, there was no way to determine which factors were to blame.

From the ages of six to nine years, Lenny received school-based speech therapy to correct articulation deficits related to his hearing problem. Judging from the continuing sound omissions described above, this was only partially successful. Full-time placement in the special education program did not begin until the fourth grade, when his learning lags had not been remediated by repeating a grade the previous school year. The new Special Day Class was instructed by a caring male teacher who attempted to boost the self-esteem of his small student group. This was a welcome change for Lenny, who vividly recalled the shame and embarrassment he endured during the early years due to taunting by his peers. He spent two school years in this special education setting, then passed on to a similar self-contained class for junior high. File notes indicate ongoing issues with impulsivity, visual-motor coordination, speech articulation, and social skills. They also suggest the possibility of a neurological condition as the basis for these complex functional issues.

Lenny enrolled in high school one year behind his age-mates, with academic skills that were now noticeably reduced. At fifteen, he was again administered a series of tests to further explain this, along with observations of "hyperactive, poorly disciplined" behavior and "sensory defects." At this point, his academic progress was described as "leveling off." He was therefore transferred to the special education program at a different high school and demoted to ninth grade status. Lenny was now *two years* behind most of his classmates. He had accepted the transfer (and demotion) in order to enroll in a special work-study program. But, when this program proved unsuccessful, he drifted away from school altogether the following year. He subsequently earned his GED high school diploma while serving time in prison.

My assessment results revealed the following skills profile:

- An IQ in the low average range
- Academic skills ranging from fifth to seventh grade levels that fell at the borderline for qualification as Specific Learning Disabilities by standard definition;
- Visual information processing averaging at age eleven and one-half, with a five-year drop to only six and one-half years in the comparable auditory channel;
- Vocabulary skills at age ten to sixteen years;
- Attentional deviations marked by omissions over time and slowed response time under high-stress conditions.

That last finding regarding Lenny's attentional deficits deserves a bit more explanation. Here, I administered the computer-based test described in Chapter Three, which yields descriptive results for Omissions (lapses of attention), Commissions (impulsivity), Response Time (speed), and Variability (inconsistency). The outcomes of this test were very clear: Lenny could attend with good accuracy for about fifteen minutes before "spacing out" and losing content; and, he needed to slow his responses down to deviant levels in order to maintain accuracy under high-stimulation conditions. These findings were highly useful to attorneys scrambling to explain how things had gone so terribly wrong during Lenny's commitment offense.

Although my knowledge and recollection of the original bank robbery remains sketchy, my understanding is that Lenny's role in it was to hold the security guard at gunpoint while his two friends carried out the rest. At some point (probably about fifteen minutes), his growing tendency to lose focus became noticeable to the guard, who started moving around. Now panicking, Lenny fired what was supposed to be a warning shot intended to scare the guard into compliance. To his horror, the bullet ricocheted off a nearby marble column and killed the man. At the trial that followed, there was no attempt to draw a parallel between Lenny's learning and attention deficits and the tragic result; thus the jury had little to deter them from imposing the ultimate penalty.

A second area worthy of brief discussion was Lenny's performance in terms of auditory processing. These subtests pointed to *severe* difficulties at all points in the processing chain. This includes the <u>Intake</u> phase, where his hearing deficit led to word distortions and substitutions; <u>Medial</u> phase errors that affected his organization and storage of material; and <u>Output</u> phase errors involving scan, retrieval, and verbal expression. His recall of single words presented in chains of up to eight items scored lowest in this battery, with some improvement once words were inserted in sentences or paired with visual content. Most important to this discussion, and to the case in general, was the fact that this single word chain test score plummeted to the mental age level of a four-year-old child. Lenny expressed surprise at his own ineptness during this subtest, and applied extra effort to improve each time a dramatic lapse would occur. Pep talks and encouragement from me helped to spur him on at these times, but the effort was too great to maintain indefinitely, and he began to lose content again. Unfortunately, in life, one rarely gets external guidance when lapses like these occur.

Lenny's appellate team now had my complete report of findings related to his learning, attention, and processing problems, along with similar reports from the three other specialists. This was all the data they needed to present a compelling case to a new jury that could negate the original penalty phase verdict and remove Lenny from Death Row. Interestingly, if the new jury found him *ineligible* for execution, there was a chance that his sentence might revert to time served, since he had now spent twenty years in prison. But, before going forward with this argument, the appellate team decided to do a dry run.

**Mock Trial**

The State PD arranged to conduct a "mock trial" before a group of ordinary people who represented the greater Chicago public. Service like this is not required or mandated under any existing jury laws, thus they hired, and paid at a decent rate, two juries of twelve people each to role play the actual event. I'm not entirely sure how these people were chosen, but I do know that one criterion for service was a working telephone. In this way, the PD screened out homeless people who might want the money, but were largely unrepresentative of the folks likely to be impaneled on the jury for Lenny's new trial. They had no trouble getting twenty-four people who wanted the pay, free lunch, and reimbursement for transportation to and from the scene, which was a mock courtroom inside a downtown Chicago law school.

I returned to Chicago to join the three other experts who would testify at the mock trial. The roles of the judge and prosecuting attorney were assumed by other Appellate PD lawyers, while the lead defense attorney played himself. The juries sat together—all twenty-four of them—and listened. We experts were allowed to stay inside the auditorium to hear each others' testimonies, which became an interesting and highly informative experience. As expected, the lead attorney went through the findings in each of our reports, and we were cross-examined as if it were a normal trial. I was able to provide test scores, including Lenny's four-year age score for the word processing test. Testimony and cross examination rolled over to a second day, but by lunch or shortly thereafter, we had concluded the mock case. The two juries retired to separate deliberation rooms which were equipped with video cameras so we could watch their discussions. The whole experience was truly fascinating for me, because I've never been on a jury.

There was one weird occurrence in this already unusual scenario, but it requires a brief back story. I have a friend and colleague in Los Angeles with whom I've worked on several local cases. I took advantage of his expertise at these times to get new pointers, since I credited him with being more savvy than myself and in private practice longer. One thing I liked about him was his knack for offering rather creative responses to questions raised by prosecutors who are trying to discredit or confuse experts on the witness stand. Once they reach a dead end trying to make us look bad academically or experientially, they usually hone in on the fact that we were *PAID* to conduct our assessments. The nasty implication here is that professional integrity flies right out the window once money enters the picture. Accordingly, my response to the accusation would usually be something like, "Yes, I was compensated for my work on this case, as were we ALL." I said this to be sure it was not lost on the jurors that both lawyers and the judge were also receiving paychecks. But my friend had what I thought was an even BETTER response which was, "My time is for sale, not my opinion." In other words, these lawyers may pay me by the hour, but they cannot orchestrate or influence my conclusions. I liked it and decided to "liberate" it for my own use. The mock trial was the first and last time that happened. Here's why.

On the witness stand, the mock prosecutor went after what each of us had been paid for our work, thus insuring that the implication of greed-based bias was heard by the two juries. Side note: Both of the female experts—myself and the Ph.D. language specialist—were paid hourly rates that were well below those of our two male colleagues. Since we basically set our own rates, this was no one's fault but our own and a great lesson for future cases: Ladies, charge what you're worth!

But back to the mock trial, where it was my turn to face the inevitable money question. I tried out my friend's answer, "My time is for sale, but not my opinion," and was quite pleased with the way it sounded. I felt smug, satisfied. This had gone just great.

Later, in the deliberation rooms, the mock juries were dissecting each testimony on closed-circuit TV and had come to my contribution to the trial. They seemed to be impressed by most of the hard data (test scores, mental age levels) I offered. But then, two women started ranting about the fact that I had said "My time is for sale ..." Apparently, they had not heard the rest of my smart aleck response, and now viewed me as no better than a common street walker. They sounded livid. Two other jurors jumped in to remind them of my ending phrase ("... but not my opinion"), but these ladies were too far gone to consider it. I was shocked, horrified, and embarrassed, but the State PD attorney told me to dismiss it because both juries had heard and received the most important part of my testimony which pertained to Lenny's test scores. Indeed, they must have, because they found him *ineligible* for the death penalty based almost solely on his four-year mental age score in the auditory processing battery.

**Actual Trial**

When the REAL trial came up a few months later, I was present and prepped to get on the witness stand, this time, without the smart remark. Lawyers from both sides presented their opening arguments as the first portion of the trial got underway. The defense argument included ballistic evidence supporting the bullet ricochet theory and a brief review of test findings of the four experts, stressing the fact that none of this had been presented at the original trial. The prosecutor then paraded the victim's still grieving family in front of the jury and began mocking the defense attorney's statements about Lenny's disabilities by dramatically whining, "*Poor Lenny M! Poor, poor Lenny M* ..." Even from the back of the courtroom I could see that her antics didn't go over well with several female jurors.

Now it was time for the jury to retire and determine whether Lenny was *eligible* for the death penalty. I was on call and ready to testify in the second trial portion which we all assumed would happen. This would be where detailed knowledge of his various disabilities would be crucial for jury deliberation regarding execution. Time passed and the day ended without a verdict, so I returned to the hotel to extend my room and airline reservations. I then used the evening to review all file materials in preparation for testimony as soon as the "eligible" verdict came forward. BUT ... in a surprise move, the jury returned around ten A.M. with an *ineligible* verdict! Lenny was basically a free man, having served twenty years for what was now determined to be accidental manslaughter. I imagine he packed up and left the prison a short time later to live out the rest of his life in peace.

Yes, sometimes we really do get it right, and *fundamental fairness* prevails.

# PART TWO

# Intellectual Disabilities

# CHAPTER EIGHT
# Tina, Confused Sexual Boundaries

Thirty-six-year-old Tina entered New York's criminal justice system as the result of rather generalized incompetence, along with ignorance fueled by tainted past experience. This intellectually disabled mother of two daughters had failed to prevent their molestation by her husband, a family friend, and her two brothers. To complicate matters further, *all* of the individuals involved in this case had been diagnosed with mild to moderate "mental retardation" in their school days, with Tina and her husband the highest functioning of the group. In the past, qualifying as one with this disorder was limited to obtaining a low score on a standardized IQ test. Not so anymore.

### Definition of Intellectual Disability

In 1992, the American Association on Mental Retardation (AAMR), now known as the American Association on Intellectual and Developmental Disabilities (AAIDD), introduced a new approach to diagnosis, classification, and support systems for individuals with Intellectual Disability (ID). This revised approach called for a standardized test of verbal and nonverbal intelligence, plus a thorough evaluation of ten functional, or *adaptive*, skills. In order to qualify as having the disorder, an individual had to 1) score 70 to 75 or below on the IQ test, and 2) show measurable limitations in at least two of ten adaptive skills which included things such as communication, self care, social and domestic skills, use of community services, health and safety, academic skills, and work. A second (2002) revision went further in grouping the ten adaptive skills into three broad "functional" areas: Conceptual, Social, and Practical. Under the revised standard, an individual had to show "significant limitations" in at least one of these three functional areas for formal qualification. Both definitions required evidence that intellectual and performance problems were *developmental disabilities* that were present prior to the age of eighteen and thus interfered with foundational learning. In other words, someone who acquired a similar condition in adulthood due to physical or mental trauma could not be classified as ID because it had no developmental effects on early learning. Before we go any further into this fascinating case, I believe a brief lesson in genetic and external causation is warranted.

### Intellectual Inheritance

In my career as a teacher and forensic consultant, I have met several families where virtually EVERYONE qualified with a formal disability of one kind or another. One of these families belonged to my student E.J., whose parents, though not formally tested, appeared to be "cognitively limited," and all six of his siblings were qualified by school-based teams to receive special education. I had another student with moderate Intellectual Disability whose sister entered my classroom the following year with identical learning issues. I soon learned that two more were waiting in the wings. Finally, a defendant and "wanna-be" Cripps gang member referred to me by his lawyer for assessment was found to function in the "mild" range of intellectual impairment. Asked about his siblings, "Terrence" reported eight brothers who had attended special education classes as children. All of them were now either dead or in jail.

How can this happen? It is somewhat understandable if *both* parents are low functioning; however, what about two perfectly normal people who have not one, but a slew of disabled kids? I met a husband and wife just like this when taking a genetics class at Children's Hospital, Los Angeles. Unbeknownst to the couple, their genetic *karyotypes* (array of genes) were evenly matched for defects, even though they were not blood relatives. As a result, all three of their sons suffered from one or more serious disorders. They finally sought genetic counseling where it was suggested they stop having children, because ALL of them would manifest some form of disability.

Genetic or other types of inborn accidents can occur at several points in the creation, gestation, and birth of a new organism. A defective gene (or genes) contributed by one or both parents is, of course, one cause of anomalies, as are cell division errors during the early formation of the fetus. Double copies and omissions of genetic material are also possible; but these are usually single occurrences with external causation such as drugs or x-rays, rather than a "trend" in the family. Other issues arise from prenatal accidents, alcoholism, inhaled or ingested toxins, and birth trauma.

What I want to stress here is that, when disabilities "run" in a family like Tina's, I tend to suspect issues from this general "inborn" category as primary causation. In my student, E.J.'s case, both parents contributed their limited intellectual structures to all seven kids, with E.J. number two in the line-up. Genetic anomalies are indeed a "crap-shoot," so you never know which child will be the most severely affected. In this student's case, his eldest brother functioned at the lowest ("severe") level and eventually required institutionalization. My student and his youngest sister were least affected, and all the others fell in between.

In contrast, "cultural-familial" causation refers to intra-family disabilities that result *after* the birth process with no known genetic contribution. This term suggests that certain cultural, religious, and/or family practices have limited the cognitive development of the children, thus creating offspring who function at lower levels than if raised elsewhere. I am referring to things such as parental neglect and abuse, sensory deprivation, dietary deficiency, poor parenting practices, and the like. It is indeed unfortunate that some otherwise normal kids acquire functional disabilities simply because they were born into an intellectually impoverished family situation. I am thinking of several infamous family groups discovered in isolated areas of the eastern part of the country. The Kallikaks are one such "tribe" of in-bred Appalachian whites who were followed and catalogued by the researcher, Goddard, in the early 1900s. What is pertinent to this discussion is that the majority of these children exhibited functional deficiencies that were linked to the substandard childrearing practices of their less than competent parents. The long and short of it is that less capable parents tend to do a poorer job raising their children to function at their inherited capacity, especially if the kids' potential exceeds their own. This is the basis for cultural-familial retardation.

Finally, it is certainly possible, even probable, that two normal parents who have one child with a severe disability can go on to have ten normal or bright children. In such cases, the disability in that one child is thought to result from a freak accident of nature that has occurred apart from genetic or familial causation. My professor at Children's Hospital used to call this "yo-yo syndrome" because it had a way of bouncing up in surprising fashion. However, when that same couple has a *second* affected child, doctors start recommending genetic counseling. The bottom line is that when you hear of a family with several disabled children, you cannot rush to judgment regarding a genetic explanation. It could be the result of cultural-familial practices or just plain coincidence.

## Tina's Early Background

Tina and her seven siblings were raised in an intellectually impoverished home by parents with limited capabilities. As a result, both genetic and cultural-familial causation were suspected as reasons for widespread cognitive disabilities among the siblings. She reported that her father, now deceased, also had children with other women, producing fourteen half-siblings at last count. One of these may have been Mike, her eventual husband, described below. Tina's father was a chronic alcohol abuser who hit and sexually abused her over several years' time. She informed her mother about the mistreatment, and the police were contacted; however, no charges were apparently filed. As Tina recalled, "They let him go. He came back." The abuse therefore continued and, at the age of thirteen, Tina became pregnant by her father. Her baby was born with severe developmental disabilities and died a year later.

Tina was identified with mental retardation (now, ID) in her early school years, and tracked into special education classes. She reportedly "loved school" and maintained almost perfect attendance at the Brooklyn public school campuses where her early special education classes were offered. For high school, she was transferred to an Occupational Training Center (OTC) in Manhattan which enrolled only special education students. Individualized training enabled her to take the subway to the downtown campus. This required a teacher-coach to shadow Tina for the first few weeks of school to insure she could negotiate the two subway transfers required for the trip. She attended the training center until the age of eighteen years, when she was "graduated" with a nonstandard diploma. It was there that she befriended Cal, a fellow classmate, who formed a close bond with her entire family that extended into adulthood.

## Current Family Situation

This brings me to Tina's family situation at the time of her arrest in this matter. Here, she, her husband/cousin, their parents, her two brothers, and both of the couples' daughters were diagnosed with cognitive disabilities that measured at mild to severe levels. Following high school, Tina had established a common-law marriage with Mike, whom she identified as her cousin. Yet, family interviews revealed longstanding confusion as to exactly who had fathered Mike. While it is possible that he was indeed Tina's first cousin through her maternal aunt, equal bets were placed on the possibility that he was actually a half-brother through the same aunt and her philandering father. Mike and Tina's daughters, ages eleven and fourteen at the time of my involvement in the case, had been tracked into special education classes since their early school years. Tina and the girls now received SSI payments as individuals with developmental disabilities, while husband Mike remained unemployed, claiming a physical ailment as the reason.

At some point, Tina's family of four became homeless and were assisted in finding a low-income apartment in Brooklyn. They took Tina's aunt/mother-in-law into their three-bedroom unit, along with several pet dogs, cats, and hamsters. Classmate Cal and his young son became frequent visitors who often spent the night. Tina proudly reported becoming a foster parent to her "Godson," Jimmy, when the boy was four years of age. The boy thereafter lived part-time in the apartment. Tina received no government support for this arrangement, asking only fifteen dollars per month from Cal as a clothing allowance for his son.

A tendency toward "hoarding" by all concerned led to extremely cramped and cluttered conditions within the apartment. Here, the family's belongings had expanded to the extent that "aisles" had to be created between the stacks. Inadequate cleanliness in the constantly used kitchen led to infestations of insects and rodents which, from all reports, found plenty of places to breed under the stacks adjacent to the aisles of clutter. One can only imagine the problems these unwelcome dwellers added to the fleas already present on the family's various pets. As the infestation began to spill outside and affect neighboring apartments, calls were made to the Board of Health which sent an agent to investigate further.

When the appalling condition of Tina's apartment was discovered, the children were removed from the home temporarily, and she was given an ultimatum: clean out the infestation of all pests to the satisfaction of the Board or the children would remain in protective custody. That lit a fire under Tina. Determined to regain custody of the girls, she accessed several large drums of industrial strength insecticide and doused the entire apartment—floors, walls, and all of the belongings in between. While this toxic remedy apparently satisfied the returning Board of Health inspector, it also brought to light the family's need for more generalized assistance. The case was hence referred to New York's Department of Developmental Services which assigned a state-compensated "homemaker" to visit and assist the family on weekdays, 8:00 A.M. until 4:00 P.M. Her duties were not restricted to simply cleaning the apartment, but included help with bill paying, arranging medical appointments, shopping, providing assisted care to Tina's mother-in-law, and helping the girls with homework. Cal's son Jimmy, now eight years old, usually joined Tina's girls for these homework sessions.

## Family Indiscretions

The open door policy in Tina's home was such that friends and relatives came and went freely for both drop-in visits and extended stays. With interior space still quite limited by clutter, it was common for everyone to move downstairs into the central courtyard of the complex to hang out and party. As such, shenanigans that sometimes morphed into lewd behavior during these largely drunken events were witnessed by any number of neighbors in the complex. Attendance at impromptu "fun parties," as well as planned birthday and holiday celebrations, typically included the whole family, Cal and Jimmy, and various drop-in acquaintances. It was at these events, as well as during routine visits to the home, that both of Tina's brothers, husband Mike, and Cal repeatedly sexually assaulted the girls. Cal's son, also victimized, was the one who finally complained of injuries to the visiting homemaker, and police were brought into the picture.

Investigations into allegations of abuse led police to question a number of Tina's neighbors in the apartment complex, where several confirmed seeing some degree of inappropriate behavior in the courtyard. These observations were confined to drunken dancing where touching violations occurred. Indeed, the only child abuse charge against Tina stemmed from a neighbor's report that she had once playfully pulled the girls' dresses up to reveal their underwear while dancing. The additional charges of child endangerment brought against the thirty-six-year-old defendant related to her failure, as the girls' mother, to prevent far more serious sexual assaults by the men. As such, these charges amounted more to *omission* of corrective behavior than direct *commission* of a crime. Tina nevertheless found herself included among the defendants in this complex case, characterized as an enabler and lesser perpetrator of child abuse.

### Multiple Arrests

Cal, Mike, and both of Tina's brothers were arrested and charged with multiple counts of child sexual abuse. Tina was also arrested, and the girls were taken to an orphanage on Long Island. Although her brothers were too low functioning to appreciate, confirm, or accurately report their precise involvement, Mike was fully able to laughingly discuss "getting after" his daughters on multiple occasions. His chatty disclosures during the videotaped police interview revealed that Tina made numerous attempts to intervene on behalf of the children to prevent the abuses that she, herself, had suffered as a youngster. Mike's candid comments regarding his wife's rather extensive efforts became crucial to the defense at her subsequent trial. Remedies she attempted here included yelling, slapping, and hitting the men; telling them "very nicely" to stay away from her daughters; shadowing the girls at family get-togethers; and finally, warning, threatening, and punishing anyone who continued any sort of hurtful behavior. At one point, Tina reportedly locked one brother inside the bathroom and refused to let him out until the girls' grandmother returned to chaperone. In addition, she chased Mike with a broom to make him behave, and counseled the girls to stay close to their grandmother whenever men were visiting.

This impressive list of interventions on Tina's part helped to alleviate, but did not end the abuse of her children. I can only imagine how continued violations by the men in her life saddened and baffled Tina as the longtime recipient of similar abuses. Indeed, past deviant experiences had left her with questions about sexual boundaries and appropriateness that went unanswered due to the absence of sex education at the vocational high school. Thus, even in adulthood, she remained unclear regarding sexual roles and taboos within a family. The defense was successful in pointing all of this out while at the same time highlighting their client's valiant attempts to prevent further injury to the girls.

Almost immediately, this complex case of intra-family child abuse monopolized the Brooklyn press, where reports described a Kallikak-like tribe of "feebleminded" sexual predators. Public outrage intensified when it was discovered that Tina's eldest daughter was pregnant when admitted to the Long Island orphanage. DNA tests revealed Cal as the father when the baby later miscarried.

Separate trials were arranged for all of the defendants, their cases divided up between defense agencies in the Borough. Although I didn't become involved in or even follow the cases pertaining to any of the others, I was informed that all of the men pled guilty and received prison sentences in the State of New York. As a result, Tina's trial became the only circus in town, with reporters and angry local citizens threatening to fill the courtroom. Fortunately, Tina's defense team prevailed in efforts to avoid a public spectacle, limiting most deliberations to closed sessions. My report was introduced at this time, along with that of a local psychologist whose tests verified my results, described briefly, below.

**Tina's Assessment**

I assessed Tina in a basement holding cell inside the Brooklyn Courthouse which happened to be right across the street from my hotel. While this was super convenient for me, it was more than awkward for a female defendant within view of male inmates in the neighboring cells. Worse yet, many of the defendants who cycled through surrounding cells delivered cat-calls and rude gestures which embarrassed and further distracted Tina. I therefore asked to move to another cell at the end of the L-shaped corridor which would afford more privacy for our task.

Tina cried many times during the assessment, mostly out of concern for her girls. She also reported feeling sad at being abandoned by her mother and aunt, both of whom blamed her for allowing the disclosure of what they considered to be a "private" family situation. Yet, even at these emotional times, Tina was easily prompted to continue. She also responded well to praise for correct answers and put forth her best effort as a result.

Tina's IQ scores of 55 to 63 were consistent with a mild to moderate degree of impairment. Tested separately, reading, spelling, and math earned first- and second-grade level scores that raised serious concerns regarding her ability to apply related skills in everyday life. These low-level scores were understandable considering that little or no direct academic instruction took place during her high school years at the OTC, where focus on job preparation was the norm. Other reductions seen in her current score profile included vocabulary that remained at seven and eight-year age levels, and information processing at ages four and one-half years to seven years. Social maturity scored highest in the entire battery at age ten years. In the final analysis, whether Tina was classified as "Educable" or "Trainable" by educational definition was a moot point now, because newer terminology focused beyond the individual, extending classification to the level of support needed to function in society. In these terms, now adult Tina would be described as an individual with a mild to moderate Intellectual Disability who required Intermittent to Limited (Levels 1-2 of 4) support services in five of the ten adaptive areas, and Limited to Extensive (Levels 2-3) supports in the remaining five.

## Case Recommendations and Outcome

Tina's assessment verified reduced mental ages in all skill categories and continuing support needs across the board. This overall outcome was useful in making recommendations for fair and effective *diversion services* in lieu of a prison sentence for this defendant. The "diversion" concept is based on the belief that cognitively disabled individuals are better served through remedial education and training programs delivered in secure community facilities than by incarceration with violent felons. What Tina needed at the time was an opportunity for self-improvement to upgrade community use, domestic skills, health and safety, and parenting. She also needed help learning a viable trade that would lead to future employment in an unskilled or semiskilled job.

It also seems pertinent to comment on Tina's sexual-social development and current educational needs in light of her deviant background experiences. For <u>any</u> client, a history of incest and physical abuse has potentially devastating effects on self-esteem. It also distorts his or her perception of behaviors which are appropriate and inappropriate between family members. Clients with normal intellects learn *incidentally*; that is, they pick up information from observations of, and conversations with others. They can then apply this information to their own experience to gauge societal norms about sexual-social behavior. Many seek private therapy from competent professionals to deal with their lost innocence and formulate new behavioral guidelines for use with their own children and families. This is a success story which is reenacted time and again throughout the normal population.

However, similar victims with cognitive disabilities are not so self-directed or intellectually competent to make these connections. For this population, incidental learning is *not* the norm, as any special education teacher can tell you. Instead, students with intellectual disabilities require direct instruction which is very concrete and specific, focused on what sexual behaviors are appropriate versus inappropriate, where (public versus private settings) they are permitted, and who make appropriate partners. Children are always described as "inappropriate" partners for sexual activity. That's why I especially like the mantra of the highly effective *Circles Stop Abuse** curriculum which was created especially for disabled learners: *"We never touch children; we only wave to them."*

As educators, we have found the need for extremely graphic teaching pictures along with detailed explanations and discussion, ample time for questions to clear up misconceptions, and "overlearning" of content in order for even minimal learning to occur. Even with this instruction, it is not uncommon for these students to miss a great deal and/or to misunderstand and internalize grossly inaccurate content. I am reminded of a story told to me by Jim Stanfield, my former professor, who now publishes teaching materials for disabled learners. It seems that staff at a state hospital for severely disabled adults witnessed sexual activity between their male clients and decided to teach a unit on condom use. Apparently this "unit" was only a simple demonstration that omitted key details that either embarrassed staff to share, or were otherwise overlooked. Consequently, a staff member later encountered two males engaged in sexual activity, with the wrong partner wearing the condom. See what I mean? Direct and graphic instruction is the key to success with this population.

What Tina needed now was an across-the-board skills overhaul, with particular counseling and education regarding appropriate sexuality. She would not get this inside any prison that I know of; thus, the diversion alternative was recommended. Having now received considerable education regarding all of the issues in the case, the Court sentenced her to just such an alternative through a public institution in upstate New York. Enrollment in this program would amount to "time served," and she would be returned to the community following its completion. So, that was the good news for Tina.

The BAD news, however, was that Tina's daughters would not be returned to her while they remained minor children. She could certainly visit them at the orphanage and could reunite her little family once the girls turned eighteen. Having spent considerable time with Tina myself, I can well imagine how devastated she was when this final blow was administered. Neither would she return to live with other family members, since the men were still incarcerated, and everyone else remained angry about what had happened.

While this is not the classic "happy ending" we might have wished for Tina, I personally have settled for knowing that she will probably develop into a more competent person who will spend many happy years with her daughters once they reach adulthood.

* The *Circles Stop Abuse* sex education curriculum is published by the James Stanfield Company, Santa Barbara, California.

# CHAPTER NINE
## Ronny, a Story of Compassion

To better understand Ronny's situation, you have to step into his sad little shoes:

*Imagine that you are a twenty-five-year-old Hispanic male with intellectual disabilities that require moderate supports in home, community, and school contexts. Suppose this diagnosis has been in place since your earliest years and you have suffered much ridicule as a result. You grew up with three brothers who are tough, mean, gang-bangers. You are not good looking, smart, or academically competent, and have no skills to compete in the world of work. You have no friends really, only the thugs your brothers drag home on occasion, and they only exploit or ridicule you. You are close to your widowed mother, a warm and lovely woman, but one who has little control over your brothers or anyone else for that matter. You walk around the neighborhood every afternoon just to appear like everyone else who is coming home from work.*

*One day you see a nice looking young woman get off the bus. You see her again the next day also, so you make it a point to be near the bus stop location every afternoon at the same time. One day she smiles at you so you begin to fantasize about having her as your girlfriend. Your brothers find out that you are smitten with her and begin to tease you. They say you are too ugly to ever have a girlfriend and the only way you ever will is to rape one. You continue your daily bus stop vigil and begin to shadow the woman to see where she lives. You discover that she and her two little girls inhabit a first floor apartment which they enter through a locked front door. Looking around, you see that the apartment also has a sliding patio door that doesn't appear to close properly thus is usually left ajar. There is no husband or roommate in sight.*

I guess you can see where this is going.

**The Crime**

More than once, Ronny visited the woman's apartment in hopes that he might make a connection that would lead to romance. Each time, he lost his nerve outside her door and returned home, dejected. His brothers began to notice these little jaunts and resumed their relentless taunting. This finally angers Ronny; he decides to take their advice.

So, one night, Ronny returns to the woman's apartment complex and climbs over the low patio wall. The interior is dark, and everyone seems to be asleep. He enters the apartment through the broken sliding door and finds the woman's bedroom at the end of a hallway. The girls apparently share the remaining bedroom, and their door is closed. Ronny has brought a few things with him that he thought might be helpful in carrying out his plan. Fumbling around with these items, he awakens the woman who, to protect the sleeping girls, refrains from screaming. Ronny uses some of the duct tape he brought to tie the woman up and cuts a smaller piece to cover her mouth. In the middle of what turned out to be an unsuccessful rape, Ronny realizes something he hadn't counted on: the woman has seen his face and will be able to identify him afterward. The end result is precisely what you're thinking: murder during an attempted rape.

### Ronny's Assessment

My assessment of Ronny verified classification as one with an Intellectual Disability due to his subaverage IQ and concurrent adaptive skills deficits. This diagnosis was consistent with school records showing placement in classes for "educable mentally retarded" students throughout his enrollment. Related deficits across the board were fully described in my report. These findings revealed that Ronny remained illiterate across all academic subjects, expressed himself using the language of a child, had no social network, had never lived independently or held a paying job, and had few leisure skills other than watching TV and playing with trucks and cars on the rug at home. This document was distributed to the attorneys on both sides, and I was called to testify.

### Testimony

The Assistant District Attorney (ADA) was angry; the police investigator was angry; even the judge seemed angry. Indeed, the ADA was itching for a quick conviction, followed by a death penalty verdict. In those days (prior to the "Atkins" Supreme Court case in 2002*) about ten percent of inmates on death row qualified as having "mental retardation." Many of these inmates didn't understand that they were going to be executed or what this actually meant. One case in Texas serves as a good example of the sort of mental immaturity I'm trying to describe. The young man in question was given his "last meal" on the day of execution, including his favorite dessert. He didn't eat the dessert, however, but put it to the side of his dinner tray. When asked about this by the guards who were about to walk him to the death chamber, the young inmate remarked that he was "saving it for later."

After the *Atkins* decision, a correct one in my opinion, inmates with Intellectual Disabilities were removed from Death Rows throughout the country. My phone started ringing with calls from attorneys in at least five states asking me to conduct assessments which could verify or rule out the condition in their clients. As you might expect, some qualified, others didn't. Ronny *did* qualify, but this was several years prior to the *Atkins* ruling. As a result, my findings had to be presented to his jury so they could make an appropriate decision as to penalty that would consider his widespread cognitive disabilities.

My testimony required a grueling three hours on the witness stand, where the angry ADA tried everything he could to negate my findings. Wasn't Ronny simply *faking* it? Didn't he *know* the possible penalty for his crime and thus *pretend* to have disabilities as a way out? How reliable were these so-called *"test"* findings anyway? And who says so? He also referred to me repeatedly as "the teacher" so as to minimize my training and forensic expertise. But the ADA's most annoying assault related to the disability category (ID) itself, where he tried to assert that the functional behaviors I had described really weren't so different from those of normal people. To do this, he glommed onto my description of Ronny "playing with trucks and cars" and feigned disbelief asking, "Don't entirely normal people own remote controlled cars that they use for leisure entertainment?" Tired at this point, I answered, "Yes, but they don't usually say 'Vroom, vroom' while they do it." Okay, it was sort of a wisecrack, but it drove my point home: Ronny was not your typical defendant, but one with childlike capabilities who had made a terrible and ultimately tragic mistake.

That afternoon, a neurologist was brought in to support my test findings and to share the results of several scans of Ronny's brain. In his ten-minute testimony, the doctor said the defendant's brain was "shrinking." That was all it took—my test data, report of findings, and testimony were instantly sanctified, believed, and trustworthy. All this time, a local reporter had been following the case, writing nightly recaps of the day's courtroom events. These articles seemed vindictive and biased to me, with weak coverage of the defense's position. That was why I felt quite relieved that the article she wrote on the day of my testimony ignored me completely. Instead the headline read something like, "*Doctor Says [Ronny's] Brain is Shrinking.*"

## Verdict and Aftermath

Ronny was indeed found guilty of the rape/murder; but in the penalty phase of the trial, the jury awarded a life sentence instead of the death penalty. Questioned about their unanimous decision, their comments mirrored the statements I had presented regarding Ronny's reduced mental capacity and pitiful prior life experiences. The reporter rushed out of the courtroom to write her nightly synopsis, which I am willing to bet included some griping about the decision. But here's what she DIDN'T see: Ronny's mother and the mother of the victim were both present in the courtroom when the verdicts were read. After the smoke cleared and people started leaving, both of these lovely Hispanic women came together in a tearful hug. They expressed sorrow for each other's grief—one had lost her daughter to murder; the other now lost her son to a life in prison. It didn't matter to them: loss was loss. This true and generous human story was never put into print, but I still think about it whenever I contemplate the meaning of *compassion*.

There are plenty of hardened criminals out there who commit purposeful crimes out of greed and/or hatred. I agree with my dad who would say that they belong "under the jail." But then there are those who bumble into crimes which escalate out of control to final tragic outcomes. My neighbor, a former ADA, used to joke that I was working for "the dark side" in cases like these. I preferred to believe that I worked for justice by insuring fundamental fairness for those who could not negotiate the complex justice process on their own.

* *Atkins v. Virginia, 536 U.S. 304*

# CHAPTER TEN
## Dee, Much-Needed Life Supports

Perhaps the best way to describe Dee and her pending criminal case is through the report, below. This document is an abridged version of the full report I presented to Federal Court. The forty-seven-year-old client was accused of aiding and abetting a Los Angeles area gang known to be involved in everything from money laundering to murder. She had met several of these middle-aged gang members quite by accident and developed a sort of hero worship for one particular woman, an alleged leader in the group. “Rita” quickly detected Dee’s intellectual immaturity and social neediness, exploiting both by directing her to carry out a number of simple, though risky, tasks. Dee was arrested along with sixteen of the gang members when her telephone conversations with Rita were picked up on a federal wire tap.

## *REPORT OF ASSESSMENT FINDINGS (Abridged)*
## *Dee, Age 47 years, 1 month*

### *REFERRAL*

*Dee was referred for assessment pursuant to an order by the United States District Court, Central District of California. She is charged with aiding and abetting several co-defendants in a RICO (gang-related racketeering) conspiracy. Department of Social Services and other professional records identify Dee as a person with Intellectual Disabilities (ID) that required special education throughout her school enrollment. Testing was completed in a single five-hour meeting which took place at Dee's Los Angeles apartment. In addition, the client's niece was interviewed to obtain background information related to her aunt's adaptive functioning. The purpose of this assessment was to determine this defendant's current disability classification, to examine any cognitive deficits that interfere with her expression and processing of information, and to document any significant adaptive deficits that are present.*

### *BACKGROUND*

*Despite being enrolled in special education classes throughout her school years, Dee has only recently learned she was diagnosed as "mentally retarded." She attended school until the age of nineteen when she "aged out" of the program with a "certificate of attendance." This client has an established case file with the Department of Social Services which documented an IQ consistent with ID classification as well as significantly reduced skills involving memory, concentration, insight, and judgment. A recent report by a local psychologist supports mild to moderate intellectual disabilities and a Social Quotient of 51 in this client.*

*After years of suffering physical, sexual, and emotional abuse as a child, Dee "ran away" with a sister after completing high school. These abuses included numerous incidents of humiliation, exploitation, and abandonment by virtually all of her family members. Even today, similar abuses continue whenever Dee interacts with her family. For example, she was recently paid three dollars to clean her sister's entire house over a full day's time. Cleaning is something she's quite good at due to years of practice in her own and other home environments. Dee is therefore relegated to Cinderella-like status by friends and family alike who exploit her kind heart and need for affiliation.*

*Upon occasion, Dee has returned to her mother's home for help completing job application forms. These efforts resulted in a succession of unskilled jobs included one sorting and hanging garments for a clothing manufacturer, and another doing stock work for a Sears store. Dee recalled once standing in for an ailing cashier at a retail store where she "fainted" when confronted for giving a customer the wrong change. Her last job racking clothing had to be discontinued when she was involved in a car accident and suffered a wrist injury. Dee now lives on a small monthly social security stipend which barely covers her rent, utilities, and food.*

*As a condition of receiving welfare, Dee was required to enroll in the GAIN program through a local community college. When it was detected that her academic skills were substandard, she recalls that "they sent me back to school" to do remedial coursework. After some time with no observable improvement, Dee was released from the class with an apology for failure to raise her achievement to the basic literacy level. The still illiterate client tearfully recalled times when she was unable to help her son with his second grade homework and felt frustrated and ineffective as a parent. She once wrote an excused absence request for the youngster which was so fraught with errors that school officials thought he had forged it himself. Dee was forced to visit the principal to prove she had written the excuse note so as to avoid the boy's suspension from school.*

*In summary, Dee has lived her life as a hapless victim, with few self-advocacy and/or functional skills in place to better her situation. Even now in adulthood, she maintains a subservient relationship in her immediate family, where they only initiate contact in order to exploit her for cleaning, cooking, or babysitting. As a result, she constantly seeks friendship and comfort from her niece's family, her son, and a few friends, mostly via telephone contacts. She appears quite outer-directed in social demeanor, readily complying with and deferring to others so as to gain their favor. But beneath this facade is a very sad woman with significant cognitive impairments who has experienced much tragedy in her interpersonal relationships. As an adult, she remains fearful and humiliated about her own ineptness.*

***BEHAVIOR DURING TESTING***

*At the onset of testing, Dee tried to act casual, even though it was clear that she had been dreading the session for some time. Many of her reactions to assigned tasks ended in tears when she could not comprehend the instructions or lacked the necessary skills to carry out the work, and was forced to demonstrate her considerable deficiencies to a stranger. Over time she began to request that the Examiner reword or repeat certain test items so as to clarify their meaning. Care was therefore taken to maximize all test scores through patient repetition of items and extending the "wait-time" where needed.*

*Intermittently, Dee became quite talkative regarding her current legal situation, expressing a strong desire to "get my life back." Since she is not incarcerated, this statement was interpreted as a wish to alleviate stress while awaiting trial. It also explained her unrealistic hope of reuniting with the "friends" who are named as co-defendants in the matter. Here, Dee played a subservient and peripheral role in the group, as substantiated in telephone conversations that were wiretapped on several occasions. The language content of these interactions will be discussed in the appropriate sections below. Suffice to say that most of Dee's statements characterize her as one with a sort of "mascot" status who, above all, sought friendship and support from these individuals. Today, she remains scared and confused about current charges which she tearfully described as, "laundry money," her arrest experience, and what lies ahead in the court procedure.*

***MULTIDIMENSIONAL ASSESSMENT***

*In order to verify and further delineate Dee's Intellectual Disability, the evaluation included a composite measure of intelligence plus evaluation of adaptive behavior across functional areas. In order to qualify with the disorder, an individual must score 70 to 75 or below on the standardized IQ test, with evidence that subaverage functioning was present prior to age eighteen. Qualifying individuals must also show related limitations in at least two of ten adaptive skill areas, including Communication, Home Living, Self-Care, Social Skills, Self-direction, Community Use, Health & Safety, Functional Academics, Leisure, and Work. Dee's functioning across these adaptive areas was determined by data from standardized tests, work samples, direct observation, and client/family interview.*

## *LEARNING STYLE PROFILE*

### *Intelligence.*

*The IQ test included a verbal component where Dee scored at only 42 and a performance section where she scored at 68. This imbalance was caused by severe difficulties recalling and expressing word labels on demand. Her composite score of 51 can be adjusted by up to +6 error points to account for test bias, yielding a functional IQ range of approximately 51 to 57. This range falls well below the population mean of 100, classifying Dee as an individual with Intellectual Disabilities that undermine insight, judgment, and decision-making.*

### *Academic Skills.*

**Note**: For the sake of brevity, outcomes across the skills covered in this section have been limited to only the most essential findings. The bottom line is that reading, spelling, and math all scored at and below first grade levels, averaging a mental age of approximately six and one-half years. Dee's *functional skills* scored a bit higher at the seven to nine year age level due to years of survival as an independent adult. A few observations regarding these latter skills will help to illustrate several of the "compensatory behaviors" she has adopted so as to appear normal in everyday activities.

***Reading.*** *Because Dee's ability to read individual words and text scored at pre-primer levels, she was given a second test of so-called "survival skills." Here, she was unable to read simple public signs such as* "push" *and* "out," *and was confused about which pictured door* *showed the store* "Entrance." *When asked how she would cope when similarly confused in public, Dee stated that she would "ask a lady" so as to avoid embarrassment.*

***Spelling.*** *Dee could not produce any dictated test words for credit. Thus, she was asked to write a few that she knew and used frequently. The short list that resulted included only love, hurt, to, the, and so. She nevertheless makes frequent attempts to write letters and cards, short notes or lists, and directions, but requires a great deal of assistance to do so. She therefore calls her niece five or six times per day to ask for help with her writing tasks. Application forms needed to obtain work or social services were well beyond her capabilities; therefore, Dee enlists the help of family members to complete them.*

***Math.*** *Dee described math as her "best" academic subject, and proudly demonstrated her ability to complete simple addition ("I love my pluses") and subtraction problems by counting her fingers or making tally marks on paper. More difficult problems that require "borrowing" or "carrying" were beyond her capability, and she is entirely unfamiliar with multiplication and division. In terms of functional application, Dee can add and subtract small, pictured quantities, find dates on a calendar, and match objects in one-to-one correspondence. However, she cannot calculate monetary sums under a dollar or make realistic monetary estimates (three boxes of thirty cent popcorn = "Nine"/Nine what?/"Nine dollars?") Neither could she tell time on a standard analog clock. Despite years of unassisted marketing and cooking, Dee had no concept of "a dozen" because she does not purchase by quantity, but by cost amount. Accordingly, she visits the Grand Central Market and specifies, "Let me have* *a dollar's worth" of whatever food she desires. This claim was substantiated by her niece, who remarked that Dee periodically buys a dollar's worth of bologna and a loaf of bread, and will live on this for a week. Because she buys only small amounts at a time, Dee has no experience with large quantities.*

***Expressive and Receptive Vocabulary.***

**Formal Test Results**. *Dee's receptive and expressive vocabulary was severely reduced for an adult, with scores sinking as low as the two and one-half year age level. This extreme language immaturity is observable in ordinary conversation, where she loses much incoming information, requiring restatement or rewording to comprehend meaning. Expressive errors in social situations demonstrate similar anomia, where Dee cannot access desired labels for all but very routine words. She also tends to repeat sentence beginnings ("I go ... I go ...") to buy time to formulate full statements. Many failed starts are observable in her informal speech, as Dee begins in one direction, abandons the utterance for a second one, and so on ("Just because of ... That things happened ... Now ... You know.") Halting starts like this made coding the average length of her separate utterances difficult, though not impossible (4.5 words per utterance in a one hundred and forty word sample.) In addition, examination of a telephone transcript containing over two hundred words uttered by Dee while conversing with Rita reveals that twelve very basic words (after, and, don't, go/going/goes, he, I, know, to, that, what, yeah, you) comprise almost half (forty-six percent) of those she routinely uses. This severe language discrepancy causes daily confusion and anxiety whenever Dee is asked to follow directions, supply answers, or formulate a cohesive story.*

*Expressive vocabulary errors demonstrated same-class word substitutions such as "chair" for* stool, *and overly simplified terms reminiscent of those provided by very young children. Dee also tended to substitute functional descriptions where labels were lacking or to skip the item entirely. For example, a* wrench *was "to fix the house" and a* wagon, *to "push stuff in it." When provided with pictured choices in the receptive test, her attention became fixed on specific parts or functions, rather than the entire gestalt of items. For example, she chose the pictured "*goat*" as the answer for the stimulus word, "*cow,*" simply because it appeared to have an udder in the drawing. When it was pointed out that several other pictured choices had udders, she had no other means of discriminating among the animals, and thus stuck with the goat as her answer.*

*These combined test findings and observations verify widespread receptive and expressive difficulties that reduce Dee's ability to accurately interpret incoming content, follow multi-step directions, and retrieve labels on command. One particular exchange during an informal discussion about her background presents a good illustration of this client's everyday receptive issues. Here, we were discussing her employment history, most of which involved jobs in the clothing industry. When prompted, "*Clothes?*" to establish the precise nature of her work at a particular store, Dee responded, "No, it's open." Extreme language immaturity of this sort was suggestive of "aphasia," a disorder usually caused by left hemisphere brain injury. Further evaluation by a licensed speech and language pathologist is therefore recommended in order to rule out or properly diagnose the condition.*

***Transcript Analysis**. To illustrate her role as a conversational partner, this evaluation included an in-depth analysis of one of the transcribed telephone calls (#6) between Dee and female co-defendant, Rita. The conversation contained over two hundred utterances by each partner, which were loosely broken down into categories such as Information Giving, Repeating Information, Asking Questions, Stating Agreement, and Supportive Comments. Peripheral content consisted of casual expressions such as greetings, expletives, and unintelligible responses. The percentage of each category for the two conversational partners was graphed for comparisons.*

*This analysis was predicated on research findings revealing that the partner with the most influence in a conversation tends to do the most talking and wields the most power in terms of giving information and directions. Looking at the percent of these "power" statements for each person, we observe that Rita's total is almost sixty-six percent, as compared with Dee's total of only eighteen percent. Prevalent utterances of the weaker conversational partner would tend to involve agreement, questions, and supportive comments, along with peripheral or unintelligible responses. These four categories total only thirty-one percent for Rita, as compared with approximately seventy-seven percent for Dee. Broken down separately, eighteen percent of Dee's utterances were questions, while forty-four percent were statements of support or agreement. The analysis makes it clear that Rita took control of these conversations in order to pass on instructions and information to her less competent partner, and then orchestrated the interactions that followed.*

*A review of these transcripts revealed what appears to be the reason Dee made phone contact in the first place; namely, to maintain a friendship network with more competent others. Here, the need for affiliation appears to be her utmost personal concern as she repeatedly voices her admiration ("You ... you're ... you are a strong woman. Very strong"; "I wanna be strong like you, man") and support for Rita's situation ("Oh, well, I thank God"; "... I was laying down right now and I prayed again.") She also seeks assurance that she is not annoying her with phone calls ("I didn't bug too much, did I?") and asks for permission to call again (... "um, can I call tomorrow?") This question is more readily understood when one considers that Dee is continually on the telephone seeking help and support from family members and acquaintances, many of whom have abandoned her precisely because she is such a pest. Her final statements to Rita contain rather pathetic proclamations of love for all concerned.*

***ADAPTIVE SKILLS***

*Testing, direct observation, and interviews were conducted in order to quantify Dee's skills across the ten adaptive areas. To qualify as Intellectually Disabled (via the AAMR definition), at least two of these skills must fall below the "average" score band of 8 to 12 on a 20-point scale. Testing revealed considerable variation in Dee's acquired skills, with four areas falling considerably below this range (Standard Scores of 4 and 5) and another four rated just below average at the 6 level. Two areas—Home Living and Self-Care—required minimal to no supports. Adaptive deficits related to her current charges are briefly discussed below.*

***Communication***. *Dee attempts to participate in interactive conversation but often requires multiple restatements and reworded content to receive communicative intent. Written language is almost nonexistent in this client, precluding both the reception of printed information and independent self-expression through this medium. Findings here raise serious questions regarding Dee's ability to comprehend court language and procedures, as well as her projected success complying with probation or parole instructions, all of which would be negatively affected by the low language skills noted in this evaluation.*

***Social Skills***. *Under optimal conditions, Dee can be socially appropriate and interacts in conversation with other adults. On the positive side, she is considerate of the feelings of others, offers help where she can, and eagerly joins into group outings and gatherings. During our meeting, she tried to maintain a pleasant demeanor and comply with directions, but was often reduced to tears due to embarrassment and frustration about her skills. Emotional inconsistency of this sort renders her socially dysfunctional at times, where it seems her nickname "Happy" is an ill-chosen one. She is also quite dependent on others for support, and appears rather desperate for human companionship and affiliation. Her niece Marissa has continued to urge other family members to treat Dee with more kindness. She is a true advocate for her aunt, and feels "like a mother to her sometimes." These factors, along with social knowledge/maturity scoring at six-to-eight years of age, negatively impact Dee's social skills.*

***Community Use***. *Dee functions adequately in her immediate community, but only for previously learned, routine tasks and outings. Here, she visits her church,* *along with local markets, and social service agencies, but cannot access new locations without direct and detailed assistance from others. To her credit, this client does manage her own financial affairs. She first cashes her monthly SSI check and pays her $360 per month rent via money order because her unscrupulous landlord has cheated her in the past. She then writes a check for her large telephone bill, with assistance from people at the bank who have come to know her as "Happy." Finally, she buys a few dollars worth of food on an as-needed basis and keeps a little cash around for bus tokens. People give her clothing on a regular basis, and she has no payments, repairs, or other upkeep to handle. What is interesting here is that while Dee is totally inept in counting coins to make change for a dollar, she has a better grasp of whole dollar amounts. This makes sense considering that counting the small number of dollars she has at any given time is far easier than counting coins that could number in the hundreds.*

***<u>Self Direction</u>.*** *Dee does not express goals or plans other than her most immediate concern of "getting my life back." With assistance and moral support, she takes hesitant but appropriate steps to get her needs met and also tends to the needs of those close to her. During testing, she could only attend to tasks for ten-minute intervals before digressing. Finally, she does not appear to initiate many activities on her own, but remains dependent upon others for direction.*

***<u>Health & Safety</u>.*** *Although Dee has learned to access medical and dental care on an as-needed basis, she continues to need prompting from others to actually do so. For example, she discovered a breast lump some time ago and called her niece seeking advice. Marissa insisted that Dee see a doctor but remains unsure as* *to whether she followed through. This evaluation must also consider Dee's unwise decision to enter into and maintain desperate "friendships" with her co-defendants in this case, as well as to endanger herself by blindly following their lead.*

***Leisure***. *Dee has few leisure pursuits due to both financial and social constraints. She watches television in her spare time and putters around her one-room apartment tending to cleaning tasks. She also attends church functions and helps the needy through their regularly-sponsored activities. Her most common pastime is talking on the telephone to anyone who will accommodate her neediness. Dee could therefore use support to develop new and varied activities that will lead to a fuller and more satisfying independent life.*

***Work***. *Dee has held several paying jobs in the past which, in most cases, were terminated when her diminished cognitive and academic skills resulted in errors. For example, giving the wrong change to a customer at a retail store resulted in Dee "fainting" and leaving the position. In another job she was too slow tagging and racking garments, and thus was let go. Unfortunately, all paid employment ceased when a car accident left her partially disabled and dependent on SSI. If she regains her health, it is believed that Dee can resume gainful employment, providing that she has initial assistance in locating a business that will be a good match to her personal style and abilities. Once so employed, intermittent monitoring on the job would be all that is needed for the client to adhere to task requirements and be a productive worker. In fact, a job would add much to Dee's life in terms of expanding her social circle and leisure activities.*

*In summary, current and past assessments support a diagnosis of Intellectual Disability, one of five developmental disorders served by the California Regional Center system. Regional Center services include not only ongoing remedial education to upgrade independent living skills, but in some cases, residential and/or counseling services in lieu of prison for nonviolent offenses. It is recommended that the Regional Center which serves Dee's geographical area be contacted in order to consider her intake into this support program.*

### *TRIAL COMPETENCE*

*Because Dee has a history of cognitive skill deficits, trial competence becomes an issue which should be considered by any court. It was evaluated using a revised Competency Assessment Instrument, where her answers were obtained using restatements and reduced vocabulary to make content as clear as possible. With these modifications, Dee appears to have acceptable understanding of RIGHT vs. WRONG, of pleas one makes in court, and the roles of those participating in the court process. For example, she understands the roles of both the defense and prosecuting attorneys in a very simplistic manner ("help me" ... "people who are against me"). She has some idea of the job of the JURY ("Look at you and study you ... see if you are lying or not") and WITNESSES ("let them know how I am"), and sees the role of the JUDGE as two-fold: "Look at paperwork/ prompt: What else? ... See if it's the truth or a lie." Dee is also well motivated to assist in the legal process, but has few ideas of how to do so effectively.*

*There were also trial competency subareas where this client had limited understanding, and these were specifically related to understanding courtroom procedures, how one should behave in court, and the possible penalties she now faces. Here, she understands that one who is found guilty of a crime may be "put away for a long time," but cannot specify where he or she would be sent to serve this time. She also remains unsure about the meaning and conditions of probation, where she can specify only "drug test" as an example. In the courtroom, Dee is aware that she must "sit and listen" and believes that they might "throw you out of court" for failure to do so. However, because she difficulty controlling her fears and emotions, Dee dreads, quite realistically, that she will cry. Her overall assessment of the court process is that people there "are talking really fast for me" and that she doesn't know "when to say 'yes' or 'no'." Thus, while some useful knowledge exists, there are also "holes" in the content that compromise her overall understanding.*

*Finally, Dee appears to have a borderline to clear misunderstanding of the charges against her ("laundry money") and has no idea of whether this is a felony or misdemeanor offense. She could explain only one (RIGHT TO A JURY TRIAL) of the CONSTITUTIONAL RIGHTS one must waive at a plea hearing. Neither could she define or elaborate on the term "PLEA BARGAIN" or its potential outcome. Her capacity to testify is severely limited, mostly due to language immaturity.*

***MIRANDA UNDERSTANDING***

*Dee also remains confused regarding the arrest process, and does not fully comprehend the Miranda warning as commonly quoted. For example, she associates the abstract concept A RIGHT with the more concrete "right turn," and thinks USED AGAINST YOU alludes to "something bad" but cannot specify exactly what that might be. Prior to our discussion, Dee did not clearly understand the idea that PRESENT DURING QUESTIONING referred to the police interview, not the courtroom. Here, like many other developmentally delayed clients, she confused the future tense of the wording ("... one will be appointed for you ...") with events to take place several days later in court "when the judge says it." Arresting officers would do well to provide the following alternative wording to clients with cognitive disabilities in the best interest of all concerned. In the final analysis, this client's various deficits raise serious questions about her ability to participate meaningfully at the upcoming trial and/or to provide a "knowing and intelligent waiver" of her rights in court or during the arrest process.*

*MODIFIED MIRANDA WARNING*

*You don't have to talk to me; it's up to you.*
*If you do, I can tell the judge what you say.*
*You can talk to a lawyer first.*
*If you can't pay for a lawyer,*
*I will get you one free.*

***ASSESSMENT SUMMARY***

*The various scores this client earned in the present evaluation make clear that she functions cognitively like a five-to-eight-year-old "concrete operational" child. This developmental level is concerned with concrete and simplistic, here-and-now desires and the short-term behaviors aimed at reaching these outcomes. As such, these individuals do not spontaneously consider all possible outcomes, or adequately plan for behavioral contingencies in interpersonal interactions. With regard to the present allegations, it is entirely possible that Dee's naive and pathetic need for affiliation resulted in her involvement with unsavory and far more capable acquaintances. The outcome of these interactions continues to shock, sadden, and overwhelm her. These observations do not preclude her future learning of more appropriate social behavior utilizing proper support systems through the Regional Center program.*

*Also at issue is 1) whether Dee can meaningfully participate in the upcoming trial process, and 2) whether she belongs in prison with nondisabled inmates. Answering these questions requires a good deal of speculation based on test scores in the current evaluation. Here, the client was found to function at developmental levels that fall well below the transition point to adult thinking; thus, ability to deal with abstract concepts is clearly dysfunctional. A trial competency interview made it clear that, while she understands some concepts and procedures in the broad sense, she does not grasp abstract information or complex content. Thus, without prior preparation and "English-to-English" interpretation of court language (words, phrases, and statements) to lower levels, it is unlikely that Dee can participate in the trial process in the same manner as do nondisabled clients. It is far more likely that she will allow others to decide her fate, agreeing or disagreeing with statements based on little more than the questioner's facial expressions and body language. It is therefore recommended that a Regional Center "interpreter" be appointed to effect two-way communication with the court in the present matter, and that her attorney and investigator devote additional time and patience to all pretrial explanations and preparation.*

*In the school setting, individuals like Dee require special consideration regarding integrated placement where they may receive poor treatment from nonhandicapped peers. Advocates for the disabled see little difference between school placement consideration and that faced by courts in determining a proper punitive environment for disabled offenders. When we consider the prison environment, we must examine carefully the ability of the disabled client to cope and function, as well as the climate for potential abuse. Although the California Department of Corrections was mandated to adhere to Americans with Disabilities Act in terms of disability identification and accommodation, they initially failed to do so. A subsequent lawsuit has now mandated that they initiate a classification and placement system for developmentally disabled inmates which may alleviate some of these concerns; however, gross discrimination continues to exist in educational and vocational programs offerings, at administrative and parole hearings, and in other aspects of daily prison life.*

*Individuals like Dee present with a variety of cognitive, social, language, and behavioral issues which require consideration in the spirit of fairness for all concerned. It is hoped that the foregoing information will be of use in determining fair punishment should this developmentally disabled client be found guilty in the present matter. If she becomes involved with the California Regional Center system, options can be made available which will circumvent prison, while at the same time providing reeducation intended to deter recidivism.*

✧ ✧ ✧

## CASE OUTCOME

TMI? Okay, maybe so, but this is only a fraction of the full report presented to the Court on Dee's behalf. As such, it omits charts and listings of test scores, specific error examples, and an Appendix of documented sources. Because it was complete and convincing, there *was* a happy ending! Dee was granted diversion in lieu of prison for her very limited involvement in the case at hand. She was further hooked up with the California Regional Center system which conducted a full needs assessment at intake. She now receives much-needed help with various life tasks and has also joined social activities that have expanded her friendship network. This is truly one case when the client's involvement in the justice system resulted in life improvements that would never have occurred otherwise. Her lawyer and the dedicated investigator (both now deceased) assigned to Dee's case were chiefly responsible for this success story due to their tireless efforts to insure *fundamental fairness* their client.

# CHAPTER ELEVEN
## Crimes of Innocence: Three Sex Crimes

Let me start by stating that, proportionately speaking, people with Intellectual Disabilities (IDs) commit far fewer sex crimes than do people with "normal" functioning. In fact, quite the reverse is true. Individuals with cognitive disabilities are far more often the *victims* of sex crimes than the perpetrators. When you read Anita's story in Chapter Fourteen, you will learn more about the naivety, gullibility, and desire to please others that make people in this disability category such excellent targets. That's why it has been estimated that a person with ID will be sexually assaulted thirteen times in his or her lifetime. These individuals also marry at a lower rate, have less sex, and produce fewer children. In this regard, I recall a married couple with ID who visited Children's Hospital in Los Angeles to find out why they had not become parents. Detailed questioning revealed that incomplete sex education had left the couple confused about the specific acts that could lead to such an outcome: they were doing it all wrong. The bottom line is that, even though a few of the chapters in this book involve sex crimes by people with ID and related cognitive disabilities, *that is not the norm*. Accordingly, please view the three vignettes that follow as they were intended; that is, to provide a view into the cognitive immaturity that defines this disability group.

## Anna, The Perfect Patsy

Twenty-year-old Anna was currently receiving services as a consumer in the California Regional Center system that was briefly described in Dee's previous chapter. If you will recall, this statewide system exists solely to serve "developmentally disabled" consumers from birth to death. The caseload at any of the twenty-one Regional Centers is open to four main disabilities plus a fifth category that serves as a sort of loophole to include similar others. Intellectual Disability is the most prevalent of the disorders served in the Regional Center system, with cerebral palsy, epilepsy, and autism following behind. A disability like Traumatic Brain Injury may be included in the Regional Center caseload under Category V, but only if it occurred in the "developmental period" prior to age eighteen and therefore disrupted early learning.

Having graduated from her high school special education class, Anna's current Regional Center goals now focused on obtaining employment and moving from her current group home to an independent living situation better suited to someone her age. Anna was therefore thrilled when her Regional Center found an upstairs apartment in the small downtown section of her rural community.

Before going any further, I must comment regarding the independent living movement that has been underway for several decades. The idea here is to "normalize" and integrate people with disabilities as fully as possible using a range of options that a team of caregivers match to their capabilities. Qualifying Regional Center consumers are then placed in single (usually) apartments, and receive drop-in visits from their counselors to insure their continued well-being. While independence is certainly a milestone worthy of celebration, consumers and their families must also prepare for certain unintended outcomes that can occur. Indeed, real independence may be accompanied by real isolation, real loneliness, and even real exploitation by others. These outcomes were exactly what Anna experienced in her first venture toward adult independence.

The apartment that the Regional Center located for Anna was wonderful in every way but one: it was right across the street from a junior high school. The kids attending this school ranged in age from about twelve to fourteen, and it didn't take them long to notice the solitary young woman who entered and exited the apartment. One day after school, two of the fourteen-year-old boys rang Anna's doorbell. They presented themselves as potential friends who wanted nothing more than to hang out on occasion. Grateful for the company, she let them in. What followed was a measured process of closer and closer contact by one of the youths, which ended in sexual experimentation. Word got out when he bragged about it at school, and the police were called into the situation.

Anna was not in custody when we met for her assessment. Instead, her attorney arranged for me to conduct it at the little house that served as this rural county's Public Defender's office. As expected, Anna continued to qualify with ID based on her reduced IQ and adaptive behavior deficits. More notable were the portions of the assessment devoted to 1) her knowledge of human sexuality and abuse prevention, and 2) her ability to stand trial as a knowing self-advocate in the justice process. The first of these areas demonstrated substandard knowledge and self-protection strategies, while the second verified weak skills to assist her lawyer. Since her mental age levels hovered between ages six and ten, I administered the *Gladys R.* questionnaire used for younger children at the time of arrest. The interview went something like this:

Q: Do you know the difference between right and wrong?
Anna: Yes.
Q: Name something right to do.
Anna: Get a job.
Q: Name something wrong to do.
Anna: Sex with kids—yuk!
Q: What happens if you have sex with kids?
Anna: You get in BIG trouble!

Did Anna learn her lesson? I think she did. I say this because the inconvenience and embarrassment regarding her arrest, brief incarceration, parental and Regional Center lectures, the current assessment, fear for the future, etc., made a deep impression that no classroom unit or teaching program could equal. Would I bet on her to abstain from a similar mistake in the future. Indeed I would, and told the judge so.

There's one more thing that the Court needed to know in Anna's case. This pertained to the fact that her averaged mental age level fell well below that of the boy who initiated the sexual contact and experimentation. In fact, if we assume that he had an average IQ, we would expect a concurrent mental age of about fourteen. So, who was running the show here? Who was the more savvy partner? And, who was being "used" by whom? To everyone's relief, the Court agreed. Anna was thereafter returned to a group home situation for a few more years, where a more effective sex education program could be implemented.

## Jimmy, Adolescent Curiosity

When Jimmy was between the ages of eight and fourteen, his mother ran a small daycare center for preschool children in their home. Because his considerable cognitive disabilities were apparent to others, Jimmy's social circle was restricted to a few other special education students who were bussed to his school. In the immediate neighborhood, however, there was little for him to do, so he hung out around the preschoolers and sometimes played with them. Considering the IQ deficits detailed in professional reports and verified in my own assessment, it is more than likely that his *mental age* was not far above that of the children in the daycare program. Accordingly, it would not be off base to imagine that reciprocal play occurred on a regular basis, the only difference being that Jimmy was struggling to comprehend the physical changes that accompanied adolescence.

Now fast forward some fifteen years, where a young woman who had attended the daycare center as a child was undergoing psychotherapy. During one session, she recalled instances of sexual abuse by then fourteen-year-old Jimmy. The therapist encouraged her to report it to the police, and she did so. That prompted a second young woman to come forward with an identical story, and Jimmy, now twenty-nine years old, was arrested. He spent the entire first night in jail crying and terrified, to the extent that staff tried to bring in medical help. Fortunately, he made bail the following day and was taken home. That was when I was called to conduct a current assessment of his skills. In addition, his attorney brought in a nationally known expert in confessions, since Jimmy's admission to the crimes had been obtained under extreme duress.

Jimmy's mother collected letters of support from teachers, neighbors, clergy, and friends, all of which verified his good character in adulthood. In fact, her son had been a model adult with not so much as a jaywalking ticket over the past fourteen or so years. I imagine that, at some point, thought was given to denying that the abuses had taken place based on his exemplary post-adolescent behavior. This would have been a weak and largely unnecessary argument, however, in that only three percent of adolescents who experiment with inappropriate sexual behavior go on to become adult offenders. Most simply outgrow the tendency to act out in this way and, like Jimmy, fall in line with acceptable norms.

The case therefore went forward with a dual focus, the first of which challenged Jimmy's "confession" based on his mental immaturity and extreme duress. This was where the other expert was expected to be of the greatest use. The second argument being forwarded by the defense attorney centered on the fact that Jimmy's reduced mental age at the time of the crimes mirrored that of his child victims. In other words, his behavior, while inappropriate, should actually have been viewed as child-to-child experimentation. Let's look at this argument a moment before continuing.

Even though most parents would discourage "playing doctor" and other exploratory touching behavior in their young children, they probably wouldn't necessarily call the police into the situation as long as the children in question were the same general age. This is another instance where size does matter, and it matters a lot. Accordingly, the charges against Jimmy had everything to do with his chronological age, possible ignorance of right versus wrong touching behaviors, and poor judgment at the time. But the Jimmy who came before the court fifteen years later had weathered this awkward adolescent period to become an appropriate, well-behaved adult. One's punishment should indeed fit his crime, but it should also consider the age, ability, and intention of the perpetrator. In this case, that perpetrator no longer existed. The court apparently agreed and awarded him at-home probation as a result.

### Ed, Deviant Sexual Experience

Ed's story began in upstate New York where he was placed in an institution for mentally handicapped individuals at the age of four. Why this was done remains a mystery, since this fifty-five-year-old man's functional behavior was now quite good in most respects, and my assessment revealed the need for no more than mild supports across the adaptive spectrum. Thus it appears that simple abandonment by a less than competent mother was the probable reason for this unorthodox decision.

In any case, Ed grew up in the institution and didn't realize he could opt for a life of independence until the age of twenty-six. That's when he signed out for the last time, migrated west, and kept going until he reached the Pacific Ocean. The new life that he established in California eventually included employment and a low rent apartment. For several decades, he worked at his maintenance job without incident and blended into the mainstream of society.

Ed's history of institutionalization nevertheless had a profound impact on his adult functioning across life domains, and sexual development was no exception. It should be noted that institutions in the 1950s and 1960s commonly omitted sex education from training options offered to clients. It was believed that such information would only lead to experimentation between patients, difficult behavior management, and possible embarrassment for all concerned. Also, to lessen the chance of pregnancy in instances where adequate supervision failed, both male and female patients were customarily sterilized during this time period, unless a guardian or legal advocate stepped in to prevent it.

Unfortunately, the vast majority of mentally disabled patients (upwards from seventy-five percent) have experienced deviant, often abusive, sexual encounters with strangers, staff, and others in institutional settings. Often, these deviant experiences are the *only* source of sexual information for these clients, and the side effects may be difficult to extinguish. In our interview, Ed indicated that he submitted to such exploitation with a male employee at the institution on four occasions in order to "get special privileges." Now an independent adult, he continued to reenact some of these experiences, and that is what led to his current charge of sexual assault.

The victim was an elderly woman whom Ed had assisted on a public bus. This occurred when the woman was mounting the stairs to board the bus and began to fall backward. Ed caught the woman and helped her get settled in the seat next to himself. She was so appreciative that she invited Ed to her home for dinner. Cooking and eating the dinner took some time, so when the hour got late, he was encouraged to spend the night on the sofa. The woman awoke in the middle of the night as Ed attempted, but failed, to rape her. During the assault, he spoke gently and apologetically as he reenacted what appears to have been a familiar deviant experience of his own. Ed might have walked away without ever being apprehended except for one thing. Having been sterilized, a lack of genetic material was detected in the body fluid evidence collected at the scene. It didn't take long to narrow down the search before Ed was apprehended.

Advocacy efforts on behalf of this defendant characterized him as the hapless victim of an institutional system that, through its defective educational and custodial programs, had doomed him to a life of failure across several functional domains. Even the elderly victim took pity on Ed at this point, and his punishment was minimized to a short-term period of incarceration.

### Summary

Once again I wish to stress that people with Intellectual Disabilities rarely commit purposeful sex offenses using threats, force, or mental coercion. Neither do they usually premeditate such crimes, nor choose victims they can "overpower" or intimidate. Instead, they seem to fall into situations where experimentation occurs as a natural course of events. Like Tina (Chapter Eight), they may be confused about boundaries and/or exactly what constitutes "inappropriate" sexual behavior. They may not understand the sexual taboos associated with family members, caregivers, or authority figures. They may not be able to differentiate emotional states such as "love" versus "friendship" and match these to people they encounter in daily life. It's cute when six-year-old Johnny likes to "hug everyone," but weird or even threatening if he continues to do so when he's twenty-six.

This is where parents, teachers, and counselors must step in to provide socio-sexual education that encompasses not only the physical mechanics, but one's relationships and the obligations they demand. As I write this, I realize how hard it is to clarify these issues in words; so, imagine how much more difficult it is for people with intellectual disabilities to comprehend all of this and then act accordingly. Throw in family, individual, cultural, and religious differences, and the problem multiplies by several factors to gigantic proportions. As parents, teachers, and advocates, we continue to do the best we can, and pray that the arc of justice will bend just a little when we fail.

# CHAPTER TWELVE
## Colin, Cruel and Unusual Punishment

Colin was a forty-five-year-old African-American man who had been housed at San Quentin Prison ever since his 1981 death sentence. He had a long history of special education as a student in both public and state-run schools. In addition, IQ scores obtained in his developmental period had been consistent with a formal ID (Intellectual Disability) diagnosis. Questions were therefore raised as to whether the 2002 *Atkins* ruling (*Atkins v. Virginia, 536 U.S. 304*) by the United States Supreme Court now applied. If continuing ID were indeed documented via standardized testing, Colin could be removed from Death Row to serve a life sentence within the regular prison population.

Colin's case was picked up pro bono by a San Francisco law firm with no experience in *habeas* appeals. They knew this and thus contracted, at their own expense, a number of doctors, investigators, and paralegals to collect data that would support the client's ID and commute his death sentence to life in prison. Because they knew very well what was at stake, they also sought consultation with one or more of the civil law firms that had successfully sued the state's prison and parole systems on behalf of inmates with cognitive disabilities. The result was simply spectacular: fundamental fairness prevailed.

## Background

I know little about Colin's commitment offense; nor did it matter anymore. That ship had sailed, water under the bridge, horse out of the barn. By the time I met him, he had already served more than twenty years of extraordinarily cruel punishment for his crime, due to his fairly substantial cognitive limitations. In this regard, the other inmates on Death Row realized long ago that Colin was easy to fool, thus periodically joined together to trick and terrify him by stating that "today is the day" for his execution. He would then tearfully wait all day for guards to come and take him away, only to conclude at bedtime that there had been a delay. Fellow inmates would sometimes extend the "joke" for several days at a time, until a guard would intervene and set Colin's mind at ease. The childlike demeanor he demonstrated here wasn't so different from his functioning prior to incarceration.

## Early Life

Colin's earliest available school records stated that he had been identified and placed in special education classes based on a tested IQ of 64. A psychologist's notation in these records indicated that his education up until that point had amounted to "a long, unrelieved experience of failure." An appended score summary focused particular attention on his reading skills which, at age thirteen, lagged at the 1.8 grade (first grade, eighth month) level. After a year in the special class, these skills were again assessed and found to have improved to grade 2.2. This means that, even with special help, Colin earned only four months' gain in a ten-month school year. Continued failure to progress academically led to a series of subsequent placements designated for students with cognitive limitations. Colin recalled that some of these classes contained children with Down Syndrome, a chromosomal disorder which typically yields mild to moderate Intellectual Disability. Teasing from siblings and neighborhood peers was commonplace and hurtful, with repeated taunts that he was stupid, ugly, and overweight.

Colin suffered one or more head injuries through accidents and physical abuse which he described as "bad beatings" at home. The traumatic insults that resulted appear to have compounded already present cognitive and emotional disorders. The most noteworthy of these incidents occurred at eleven years of age when Colin was struck and dragged by a car. The accident broke his front teeth and left him lying in a hospital bed, dazed and delirious. Subsequent events which have been linked to reduced brain function in the now adult client include episodes of glue sniffing as a young teen, being struck in the head with a bat in his mid-teens, and kicked in the forehead by a cow a few years later. Thus, it came as no surprise that a subsequent neuropsychological evaluation diagnosed "brain injury—primarily affecting the frontal and parietal lobes" due to these multiple head traumas.

Due to deteriorating family conditions, various public agencies became involved in out-of-home placements over this client's teen years. These typically recognized his ongoing need for special education services and placed him accordingly. A brush with the juvenile justice system connected Colin with a caring probation officer who observed him as "unusually dense and slow" as compared with other wards who came from similar backgrounds. He therefore investigated local placements for "mentally slow children" that could accommodate Colin's special needs. Yet, despite this intervention, the youngster's learning rate appears to have stalled, and the gap between actual achievement and grade placement widened.

Teachers came to expect and excuse reduced skills in the cognitively impaired youth; thus, grades of "D" across academic subjects at one court-ordered placement were rather oddly paired with comments that Colin was "working at expectation." Several of his former teachers explained their reduced expectations in hand-written memos. One of these acknowledged that he possessed "many of the characteristics of the mentally retarded," including attentional and perceptual lags, and an inability to deal with abstractions. Another noted that, over the summer, Colin had "slipped way back," losing skills that appeared to be in place the previous June. This astute observation aptly describes the *durability of learning* issue that plagues special educators seeking long-term gains in their students. In fact, this commonplace erosion of previously learned material is the main reason that school districts at one time mandated summer school for their cognitively impaired students.

Despite his dismal record of failed achievement in all school placements, Colin reported receiving a high school diploma while detained at a juvenile detention facility. In our interview, he could not explain how this came about, and had no recollection of academic coursework while enrolled there. That, plus his ongoing illiteracy, suggested that the diploma was earned via the "differential standard" allowed special education students with current Individualized Education Programs (IEPs) in place. This once common practice allowed students with documented disabilities to "graduate" (or alternatively, to earn a Certificate of Attendance) while pursuing learning objectives more in line with their reduced skill levels. Regardless of its precise meaning, Colin's self-reported diploma indicates the completion of twelve years of formal education.

**Assessment**

My assessment of Colin took place inside the visiting area of San Quentin's Death Row housing unit where, for some reason, guards limited our time in the plexiglas booths. Accordingly, two return visits were needed to gather enough hard data to accurately describe his current limitations. Over the three visits, I managed to conduct a standardized battery of tests that yielded the flat profile of reduced skills listed below.

- Reading and spelling skills stalled at first grade levels; math better developed to grade four;
- Functional (community) literacy in both reading and math falling at the "lower extreme" for an adult subject;
- Vocabulary scoring at eight-year levels (expressing words) to fourteen-year levels (understanding the words of others);
- Auditory information processing reduced to the level of a six and one-half year-old child;
- Independent living skills rated as "severely sub-average" across the full battery.

The omission of a current IQ score was purposeful, in that abundant file data existed to verify severely discrepant scores in Colin's developmental period. Additional findings regarding his early adaptive skill deficits were obtained from interview comments during visits with family members, along with declarations and file data from more than a dozen lay and professional sources. This information was crucial for ID diagnosis per the AAMR 2002 guidelines. It also tells a very sympathetic story of what his former teacher described as Colin's "long, unrelieved experience of failure."

**Adaptive Skills**

To really understand Colin's everyday life skills and abilities, one had only to talk with those closest to him; namely, his sister and two paternal aunts. Now deep in the appeal process, the law firm spared no expense to facilitate these visits, and thus provided an investigator who drove me to meet with them. I also took advantage of a rare opportunity to obtain off-hand comments from a San Quentin guard who became chatty one day as I awaited entry. Here, having noted the name on my inmate call slip, he spoke briefly about Colin's need for special handling within the unit. All of these comments, plus those taken from the sworn declarations of other family members, two psychologists, and his former probation officer, were included in Colin's report in order to paint a clear picture of his functional limitations. The highlights are presented below using the following cast of characters:

| | |
|---|---|
| Colin's Sister – | Jane, interviewed at length in the motel room that had become her cluttered studio apartment in downtown Oakland; |
| Paternal Aunt #1 – | Ann, interviewed at her standard Oakland apartment complex; |
| Paternal Aunt #2 – | Lill, interviewed at her large home in the Bay Area suburbs; |
| Probation Officer – | Mr. M, comments taken from file documents and his sworn declaration; |
| Former Stepmother – | Pam, comments taken from sworn declaration; |
| Chatty Guard – | Guard B, casual comments during my San Quentin visits. |

**Communication Problems**. Several family members recalled speech and language deficits in Colin's childhood. One of these was Aunt Ann who verified speech problems that lasted into his teenage years. She also described her nephew's difficulties accessing labels for everyday objects, and provided "car ... table ... and chair" as typical examples. Expressive problems like these often led to gestural responses (e.g., pointing) in place of more age-appropriate labeling, and caused extreme frustration for both Colin and his listeners. Aunt Ann also recalled times when her nephew "pretended to understand" simple instructions provided by his mother so as to avoid getting in trouble. At these times, the puzzled look on his face made it clear that his head nodding response was merely an attempt to feign understanding. Finally, Mr. M, Colin's former probation officer, observed similar problems giving instructions to his ward, and thus resorted to using only "simple questions and answers" at the youth's reduced language level in their interactions together.

**Academic Problems.** Colin's functional application of simple academic learning had been consistently problematic over time, with related issues reported by both professional and family sources. For example, Pam, Colin's former stepmother, recalled that even as a teenager, he remained illiterate across subject areas. She observed instances in the home where his ongoing problems telling time led to "confusing minutes with seconds" and being "way off when estimating blocks of time." Sister Jane, a year Colin's senior, verified problems counting money during their shopping trips together. She vividly recalled a time when Colin put one ten and two twenty dollar bills on the counter for purchases totaling approximately ten dollars. When she asked him, "Brother, what are you doing ... are you crazy?" the embarrassed youth responded that he was "leaving a tip." Missing money concepts continued to be problematic throughout adolescence, leaving Colin at the mercy of vendors and shopkeepers. Jane recalled another time when her then teenaged brother handed the cashier a one-hundred dollar bill for a forty-six dollar purchase and stated, "You can have the change."

Likewise, Aunt Ann spoke of the need for shopkeepers to assist Colin in identifying items he could not read; she also verified her sister Lill's observation that *dyslexia* appeared to "run in my family." The reading problems both aunts referred to spanned three generations and affected several of their siblings, including Colin's father. Ann observed that their nephew was passed on in school despite the fact that he couldn't "read, write, or even count." As he matured, Jane continued to assist him with purchases and telling time, and other family members helped him complete job application forms.

**Problems with Self Direction.** Aunt Ann recalled her nephew's helpless responses despite a growing interest in finding a paying job. Here, when asked what he wanted to do for work, Colin would merely shrug his shoulders. Immature indecision like this, along with his inability to determine the small steps needed to reach a goal, and his "extremely short attention span" greatly undermined the youth's self-direction skills. Several other family recollections suggest that long-term problems in this area had resulted in "following and doing the bidding of other people" (per stepmother Pam). Interestingly, many of Colin's problems with self direction were resolved in the prison setting, where he was always on "controlled movement" that followed a fixed schedule (per Guard B). As a result, he received enough assistance, monitoring, and external prompts that Self-Direction became a non-issue in the prison environment.

**Immature Social Skills.** A 1992 psychological evaluation noted that Colin "lacks even the rudiments of polite social conventions" due primarily to experiential neglect. The professional who wrote this report further noted this client as "distant and cut off from other people" with "extreme difficulty experiencing feelings." An even earlier report from a juvenile detention facility evaluated him as one whose personality development had been "seriously retarded," resulting in "little awareness of the cause and effect of his behavior." In his declaration, Probation Officer M added his own amazement at Colin's gullibility, which led him to "respond to his peers without thinking" and do "stupid things." Likewise, Aunt Ann observed shyness and awkwardness in social interactions, as well as gullibility which was well known around the neighborhood. Due to this particular feature, Colin was repeatedly duped by other kids who were aware that he was "easily led." Finally, at home, relatives like his stepmother Pam described him as socially immature, with leisure interests "in keeping with someone who was much, much younger." In this regard, Colin liked to listen as she read stories to her children, who were some ten years younger than he was; he also "enjoyed watching cartoons with them, particularly Superman and Popeye."

**Late Developing Self-Care Skills.** These skills were a long time coming according to Colin's probation officer and the family members who provided sworn declarations. For example, Pam had to remind her stepson to take baths, comb his hair, and brush his teeth even as a teenager; and Mr. M had to make sure he wiped his runny nose. Aunt Ann further recalled that Colin could not tie his own shoes until the age of twelve. In our interview, he claimed to participate fully in routine self-care activities available to him at the prison. This may have been true, since shower schedules and other routines were monitored by staff.

**Daily Living Problems.** Colin was only able to provide partial answers when posed hypothetical problems that could crop up in a home environment. For example, if his house was always either very hot or too cold, he would "fix the thermometer" on his own rather than calling an expert to remedy the situation. Other responses to posed situations offered similar half-solutions that might provide a temporary fix, but would not truly remedy the problem. Sister Jane recalled a few stories about Colin's very limited cooking skills. Here, he was able to heat hot dogs on the stovetop, but "burned himself on the stove many times trying to cook the food." On one occasion, Jane found Colin placing an egg, whole and unshelled, in a frying pan and turning on the burner.

**Problems with Community Use.** Colin was able to negotiate his way around his current prison "community," but only because he was "always escorted or on controlled movement," per Guard B. He was also able to access medical services for his periodic complaints; but again, this was because staff had learned not to expect him to fill out request forms on his own. Instead, medical technicians visited Colin's cell on a regular basis in order to help him complete the necessary forms. In her declaration, Jane outlined a few similar problems her brother demonstrated as a youth in community contexts. For example, up until the time he was eight or nine years old and "should have known better," he still "walked right out in the street, not looking to see if traffic was coming." Other community integration activities were undermined by his illiteracy and were therefore reduced to "reading" pictorial material and rebus symbols on public signs.

**Problems with Health and Safety**. Presented with hypothetical situations involving health and/or safety issues, Colin named proposed actions that *began* to solve the problems. For example, he said, "[I would] lay down and try to stay calm" when experiencing chest pain, but did not go the distance to access additional professional help (in the referenced case, calling for emergency medical help). It was feared that these short-sighted actions would lead to negative consequences for one with his cognitive limitations. A few of these answers revealed the extent to which this client had come to rely on external assistance in the closely monitored prison environment. For example, when asked how he would remember to take medication "three times a day" without such assistance, Colin remarked, "See, that's the problem—I did that." He then went on to explain that he "kept forgetting" to take his prescribed medication during the day, so he took all three doses together at night.

**Lacking Leisure Skills**. According to family reports, Colin had no age-appropriate hobbies or interests as a youth. His stepmother recalled that whenever card games were played in her home, "It took Colin a long time to learn the rules, so I leaned over and helped him with his cards when it was his turn to play." Even as a teenager, he watched cartoons with Pam's young children; and Aunt Lill observed that "Howdy Doody" was another of his favorite TV shows. Likewise, Probation Officer M noted that Colin "was not smart enough to play along" with other wards. Peer problems while in custody apparently led to quite a bit of isolation, and he never learned good social interaction skills as a result.

These and other interview comments were considered along with formal test results in academic achievement, functional literacy, and language competence in determining ongoing adaptive deficits across the three broad areas (Conceptual, Practical, and Social) outlined in the 2002 AAMR definition. The sworn declarations of family members and others verified the enduring nature of Colin's adaptive skills deficits. Results do indeed show strengths combined with limitations, and also verify that proper supports in the prison environment have resulted in fairly good skills in certain practical areas. The overall picture, however, supports the second criterion for ID identification and thus challenged the death penalty under the *Atkins* ruling.

## Case Outcome

Colin's appeal case was never brought to court because the numerous professional reports, declarations, and school documents laid out his case loud and clear. He had indeed been diagnosed with the developmental disability in childhood and continued to qualify as one with Intellectual Disabilities as an adult. Accordingly, the *Atkins* ruling applied, convincing the prosecutor and judge alike to remove him from Death Row. No one would disagree that Colin should remain incarcerated for his commitment offense, but neither should he live in daily fear that execution is imminent. This was a decided victory for disability advocates fighting for the fair treatment of affected individuals.

# CHAPTER THIRTEEN
## Earl, Toxic Exposure

To understand Earl, you would have to know something about his childhood in a town I'll refer to as "Mining," Oklahoma. I chose this name because that is what the town was known for—*mining*—which had been going on unrestricted for more than a century. The heaps and piles of residue left behind from ore excavation was a toxic blend of lead, cadmium, and zinc-contaminated dust called "chat." The discovery of cave-in risks, groundwater contamination, and health effects associated with the chat piles and subsurface mine shafts resulted in the area being designated as a Superfund Site by the U.S. Environmental Protection Agency in 1980. Thereafter, Oklahoma and two neighboring states similarly affected by mining at this same Superfund site took steps to remedy the situation by cleaning up the area. Despite this effort, a 1996 study found that thirty-four percent of the local children still suffered from lead poisoning which could result in lifelong neurological problems. By the time that study found its way into print, then forty-eight-year-old Earl already presented a perfect example of this outcome.

## Background

To obtain background information in this Death Row appeal case, an investigator working for the Federal Public Defender's office took me on a little road trip to Mining. The idea here was to see the environment Earl grew up in and to interview Aunt Alma, his only living relative. At the time, Mining was in the process of becoming a "ghost town" due to governmental efforts to relocate families with children under six years of age. Families with children age seven and above were on their own, so their slow voluntary exodus was only partially underway at the time of our visit. A subsequent (2008) tornado that leveled 150 homes sped up the process, diminishing the population from over 1,600 per the 2000 census, to 20 stalwart souls who refused to leave at any price.

The investigator and I first stopped at the local cemetery and got out of the car to peruse the headstones. Quickly calculating the birth and death dates on the markers, I realized that few of the people buried here had lived to be over fifty. Okay, I didn't see every single headstone, but you get the idea: People tended to die young in Mining. Then I saw why.

I was expecting "chat piles" of perhaps six to eight feet in height, but instead found some over two stories tall and spreading the width of an entire city block. Indeed, Earl's childhood home was directly across the street from a several block chat accumulation that looked like a moonscape corridor through building-sized dunes. The term "attractive nuisance" is highly applicable here, in that the chat resembles lovely white beach sand, ideal for climbing, digging, and coasting fun. Because of this, signs were posted on doors, walls, and telephone poles all over town warning people to wash their hands often and use available doormats before entering local businesses. Ironically, some of these signs had been made by children attending Mining's elementary school, emblazoned with slogans like *"Don't put lead in your head—wash your hands!"* Yet, as we drove out a long country road to visit Earl's

Aunt Alma, we passed a homestead with three small houses arranged haphazardly before a huge chat backdrop. I whipped out my drugstore instant camera in disbelief to take a very bad picture (sorry, no zoom feature) of two tricycles their children had left in the chat when they went inside for lunch. I still have those photos, by the way, and got chills revisiting them to write this chapter.

One more note regarding our Mining visit will tell you something about the stubborn toxicity of the chat dust clinging to virtually every surface in the town. Here, we saw stray dogs and cats ambling slowly across, and sometimes just *sitting in*, the road, staring blankly at our car. Being so low to the dusty ground, they had apparently ingested enough lead residue to cause neurological problems similar to those found in humans. This was verified by ladies at the local luncheonette who added that these strays broke out with blisters whenever it rained, and the dust soaked into their paws. And, yes, we did take our lives in our hands by stopping for lunch at the only bright and clean spot in this failing town. To minimize the health risk, we ordered things that came prepackaged or canned, with no chance they were grown locally. The friendly waitress put our tuna-on-Wonder Bread and Coke-in-a-can lunches down on the table along with a nice little treat—French fries that were "home made right here in our country kitchen!" We thanked the waitress kindly and buried them under the lettuce we had removed from our sandwiches. Leaving town later, we passed a huge corn field only a mile or two down the road, which undoubtedly drew water from Mining's toxic aquifer. I shudder to think how far reaching these effects were, and probably still are, on the developing brains of local children.

So, this is where Earl spent much of his life prior to taking up residence on McAlester Prison's Death Row. He was born to a single mother who, according to hospital records, was herself suspected of having a developmental disability. He began elementary school in Kansas City, placed in a special room for kids then labeled as "slow learners." A subsequent move across town mistakenly landed him in a regular class where the teacher quickly discerned, "(Earl) comes from a special room ... he cannot work at this level." His IQ score at that time was listed as 73, which falls at the borderline for formal ID (Intellectual Disability) qualification today. It is not known whether this IQ reduction was simply hereditary, or the result of a car accident that occurred when Earl was five years old. The three-car collision had rendered the boy unconscious, leaving him hospitalized with a blood clot, seizures, and recurrent headaches.

A short time later, Earl and his mother moved to Mining. Since the local elementary school did not have special education classes at the time, the boy was enrolled in the regular program and promoted a couple of grades based solely on his physical appearance. In this regard, Earl had now grown several inches taller than most other children, but didn't have the performance skills to match. A hostile teacher only added to problems that soon became well known throughout the small school. Earl's sister recalled that when she entered his same classroom the following year, the teacher remarked, "So, you're the retard's sister!" Little wonder that, after suffering two years of daily humiliation and taunting abuse, Earl dropped out of school altogether.

Asked about his childhood pastimes, Earl fondly remembered building a "fort" complex in the chat landscape across the street from his house. Chat play continued throughout childhood and into early adolescence, when his solitary excavation projects were abandoned to ride bikes or wagons over and through the giant dunes. Although he was not yet fifteen when he left school, Earl managed to get work with one of the mining companies hauling ore up shafts to the refinery. It was therefore suspected that his continuing ID resulted from a combination of internal (heredity) and external (brain trauma) factors that were exacerbated by years of exposure to the toxic mine residue. Indeed, last tested, Earl's IQ had dropped several points to a score of only 66.

## Assessment

Just after the Supreme Court's 2002 *Atkins* decision, I was contacted by the Federal Defender's Office in Oklahoma and asked to test six men on Death Row at McAlester Prison. The defense team knew not all six would qualify as "mentally retarded" under *Atkins*, but believed they could present a good argument that Earl, at least, fell into the class of prisoners now excluded from execution. As an aside, my testing of the six men revealed two with fairly clear ID qualification, two in a "borderline" range that was worth pursuing, and two whose executions were carried out almost immediately. One of these was Gary, a talented artist who shared several of his pencil drawings with me during our evaluation session. This is the sort of interaction that reveals the true humanity of a person, and reminds me that we are *all* so much more than a single deviant act.

I know very little about Earl's commitment offense other than the fact that it involved the murder of a female acquaintance. Neither did I need to know: I routinely assumed all of my clients were guilty and just moved on from there. The McAlester Prison staff turned out to be very hospitable, affording us a private room and all the time that was needed for assessment purposes. The tests I conducted were charted by mental age, grade level, and standard scores in order to paint as true a picture of Earl's functioning as possible. Here are those findings in a nutshell.

- An IQ falling between 67 and 69, which was consistent with ID classification;
- Reading and spelling scores falling below the first grade level and a functional literacy score that bottomed off the test and was thus listed as <55;
- Math skills developed to the fourth-grade level, and quantitative literacy at 78;
- Oral language skills equivalent to that of a nine to eleven-year-old child;

- Information processing skills like those of five to seven-year-old children;
- Social maturity just below age nine, and a fund of basic information at age twelve.

On the positive side, Earl had developed age-appropriate adaptive skills in the two areas of Home Living and Social Skills; however, the remaining eight areas demonstrated independent function similar to that of children between the ages of five and nine. These observations, plus a full scale Independent Living score of 65, easily satisfied the second criterion for ID classification. A few observations here will help to describe everyday functioning for an adult with these skill deficits.

Total illiteracy was at the heart of Earl's most debilitating adaptive problems. Having been embarrassed so many times in school and community contexts, he had long ago given up trying to "sound out" even the simplest words. Accordingly, the fifty-four-year-old client could not read signs directing him to local stores or services, follow simple directions, or read street names in order to find required addresses. Neither could he specify when a machine was *"Out of Order"* or identify the *"Closed"* sign on a restaurant door. Asked how he would determine whether a store was open for business, Earl replied that he would try the door and, "If it don't open, I know it's closed."

Earl had nevertheless held several paying jobs prior to incarceration, including one as a driver for a commercial moving van company. Records indicated that he had obtained his driver's license for this job via oral examination. Asked to explain how he had managed to locate the addresses for furniture deliveries, he replied that he elected to drive the van while his partner read directions and street names to him. Severe reading problems had also prevented Earl from ordering a meal using a standard menu, so he would instead request common items such as bacon and eggs or simply point to pictures of food items. At this literacy level (Level 1 of 4), there is no way this client could use public vending machines or ATMs without assistance, and he had never even attempted to complete bank forms in order to deposit or withdraw money.

Finally, the prison is also a "community" of sorts, where Earl reported being unable to fill out the forms necessary to obtain medical or dental appointments. He was also hesitant to use the commissary to purchase snack food items to keep in his cell. Neither could he read incoming mail without help from guards or other inmates. In some cases, this can prove embarrassing or even dangerous, so Earl had elected to limit written communication from his few remaining relatives. Legal information related to his impending appeal was therefore delivered in person by visiting lawyers.

## Appeal Trial

I reviewed numerous other professional documents in preparing for testimony at the trial appealing Earl's death sentence. These documents included a recent neurological assessment, records from two state hospitals, school records from both Kansas City and Mining, prison records, and a psychological evaluation prepared just prior to his original trial. I also had access to the testimonies of Earl's sister and a childhood friend, a local psychologist, and two state investigators assigned to his case. I was prepared to present my findings along with data from all of these sources at the trial which was scheduled to take place just prior to Labor Day in a small Oklahoma city. That was when things began to get weird.

I arrived in town on Wednesday, prepared to go on the witness stand the following day, only to be told there was a delay. It seems that the local psychologist had some sort of conflict, so my testimony was being pushed back until Friday. Hanging out in the small town was extremely boring, so Earl's lawyers arranged a visit to a boot store (I didn't buy any) and a group dinner at a local restaurant that served the most enormous platters of food I have ever seen. I found out that Oklahomans love their meat and consume whole slabs of it along with side dishes that were meals all by themselves. Meanwhile, the trial delay continued, so I was sent home for the holiday weekend on Friday and ordered back to testify on Tuesday at 9:00 A.M. sharp.

But, I wasn't called to the stand on Tuesday, or Wednesday, or even *Thursday* as delay after delay continued. The apologetic defense team therefore decided to fill my time with the very enlightening excursion to Earl's hometown described earlier in this chapter. It wasn't until Friday morning that I was finally called to the witness stand, and things got fifty shades weirder.

Earl's attorney had spent about an hour methodically and effectively going through my report when she suddenly turned away from the judge and projectile vomited all over the defense table! The court took a recess while everyone scrambled to get wet paper towels to clean up the area as best they could. That was when I heard several jurors who apparently thought the young female attorney was suffering with morning sickness, remark, "Bless her heart." When I resumed the witness stand, a few wrinkled noses in the jury box convinced the judge to move the trial to a different courtroom, so we hastily completed my direct examination and recessed until after lunch to find one. It was now 2:00 P.M. and there was a lot of ground to cover before my five o'clock flight. The prosecutor knew this and was purposely dawdling, so I called the airline and arranged a later flight.

It pains me to recall all the corners that were cut to present my remaining testimony to a jury that very much needed it to do their job. You see, in Oklahoma, juries of ordinary laypeople made the final decision as to whether the person in question did indeed suffer from a formal Intellectual Disability. And I'm reasonably sure that there wasn't a doctor or any other professional with knowledge about ID among the nice country folk that made up the jury. This is why it infuriated me when the judge, while admitting that the delays had not been my fault, instructed me to provide shorter answers to move things along. I don't think I have ever felt that level of outrage mid-testimony, since a man's very life was at stake, and I had data that was crucial to the decision at hand. In the end, we managed to get through a smug cross examination by the prosecutor that limited my full answers, plus a very rushed redirect by the defense attorney, just before 6:00 P.M. The investigator and I fled the courtroom to make a dash for the airport.

**Decision**

The rest of the story was told to me by the defense attorney who had charmed the jury earlier with her dramatic illness (which, by the way, wasn't morning sickness. She had a beautiful baby girl a year or two later that had nothing to do with the courtroom debacle.) She presented the case for deliberation immediately following my departure which would have made it dinner time on a Friday night in a food loving town. She knew the jurors would be anxious to go home, so she begged them to—*if nothing else*—review Earl's elementary school file to see that he was diagnosed with intellectual disabilities long ago as an innocent child. It's doubtful that they did this, however, because in the one-hour deliberation that followed they bought and ate a pizza and then returned with the verdict: Earl was <u>not</u> mentally retarded. No test scores proved it to them. No teacher or hospital records. Not the current testimony of a neuropsychologist, a psychologist, or myself either. No, Earl wasn't appreciably different from the ordinary men they encountered in everyday life. He was therefore returned to Death Row, but his gutsy defense team vowed that the case wasn't over.

I was subsequently provided a transcript of my rushed and abridged cross examination and asked to write an addendum report explaining all of the things I would have added if given the chance to do so. This was forwarded to the next level of the Oklahoma Appeals Division which arranged for a new trial in a different location, before a new judge. To my knowledge, that trial has yet to take place. Suffice to say that executions cannot go forward as long as appeals are pending, so preparing for these procedures can be drawn out for years. Until then, Earl's fate remains in limbo as the appeal effort charges on.

# CHAPTER FOURTEEN
# The Rape of Anita

By now you have undoubtedly realized that the vast majority of my work was on behalf of defendants, inmates, and parolees whose disabilities required explanation to insure their fair treatment within the justice system. At least that's how I saw it. However, my reputation among local prosecutors was slightly different, where I was called a "bleeding heart" advocate (and worse) on more than one occasion. But think about it  why would a D.A. want to hire someone to explain disabilities in someone they were *prosecuting*? If anything, such information was usually shoved under the proverbial rug as they portrayed these hapless defendants as brilliant masterminds undertaking premeditated crimes. I will append a little vignette at the end of this chapter that will illustrate this point. But for now, suffice to say that I was not at all popular with the D.A.'s office and therefore received only a handful of referrals from this source over the entirety of my career.

This is why I was surprised and pleased to receive a request from the DA's office to assess a disabled victim who had been raped at a local junior college. "Anita" had multiple handicaps including Intellectual Disability (ID) and mental illness. She lived with her grandmother/guardian, and had attended special education classes throughout her entire school experience. When she entered high school, her grandmother saw the potential for additional issues to crop up since Anita was a pretty girl and friendly to strangers. So, this savvy grandma reconvened the IEP (diagnostic and planning) team and persuaded them to assign a one-on-one aide to Anita throughout the school day. This person's job was to act as a coach and tutor, plus monitor her actions at all times, in and out of the classroom.

Under federal law, special education students have a legal right to attend public school programs until they turn twenty-two years of age. The usual process is to "graduate" from the high school campus at eighteen and then enroll in an adult program at another location. This could be a nonpublic school, an advocacy group or association, a junior college (JC), or some other agency which is vendored by the local school district or Regional Center to provide these "transition classes." Anita was accordingly enrolled in an all-day class that was held on the campus of a local JC. The one-on-one aide went along with her at district expense as specified in the current IEP. This document is a <u>contract</u> between the school district and parent which guarantees specific services to a student. The IEP contract cannot guarantee academic or behavioral *outcomes*, since these depend on many factors outside of the school's control; but *services toward desired outcomes* are not only guaranteed, they are mandatory. This is why there could be no doubt that the one-on-one aide should and would be at Anita's side to prevent the inevitable. But she was not. Here's what happened.

### The Crime

Anita asked to go to the restroom one afternoon and was excused to do so. The aide was available but for some reason didn't go along. Why not remains a mystery to me. How unthinking could she have been to let Anita roam around an open college campus on her own, especially considering that the sole reason for her employment was to supervise this one single client. But she did. On her way back from the bathroom, Anita encountered a young man she had never seen before. He called her over, and she complied. He then lured her under the stairs around the side of a building and raped her. The assault was fast and violent. Anita realized she was bleeding and that her pants were ripped, so she went back to the classroom to get assistance from her aide. Asked what was wrong, Anita said only that a bad man had "hurt her" under the stairs. It took several more questions before an approximation of what really happened came out. She was taken to a state-of-the-art medical center where tests were conducted, DNA obtained, and pictures taken. A criminal case was then filed, but there were no leads, and no perpetrator anywhere in sight.

Let me add here that this is why people with ID make the perfect victims of such crimes: they are notoriously bad reporters. Anita's description of the rapist was so vague that few males were *ex*cluded: he was dark-skinned, under forty, and wore a hat ... backwards. Worse yet, she could not describe what he actually *did* to her, nor understand the potential consequences. Anita did not become pregnant from the assault; however, several months later she tested positive for Hepatitis, a condition that precluded her from living in her current Regional Center group home. This unfortunate outcome was the last straw and ultimate reason that Anita's grandmother filed suit against the school district for failing to carry out the terms of the IEP contract. She therefore had both civil and criminal cases pending concurrently, and my report was intended for use in both of them. Unfortunately, Anita's vague description of her rapist never led to an arrest, so the criminal case was eventually abandoned. Her civil suit against the school district did go forward, and resulted in an undisclosed monetary settlement. This money would help to provide a future board and care option when Anita's aging grandmother became unable to continue as her primary caregiver. Meanwhile, her social network, which had once contained all of the other residents of the group home, was decimated, leaving Anita somewhat isolated and depressed.

## Aftermath

You may be interested in a couple of follow-up events related to this story that portray the cognitive immaturity of this and other disabled victims. The first occurred about two weeks after the attack when information about the rape finally leaked out, and a local TV station ran a news story about it. Anita happened to be watching television when the story broke and called her grandmother to the room, saying, “My school is on TV!” As the reporter recounted the details of her very own assault, Anita added, “Oh! Someone has been raped!”

The second occurrence requires a little factual foundation. It seems that Anita had several times expressed a desire to one day have a baby of her own to love. She had been carrying around a lifelike infant doll a little too often for Grandma’s comfort and started seeking information about how, exactly, one gets a baby. When she continued and expanded this line of questioning after the rape, Grandma had an idea. Yes, it was overly simplistic, but it solved the immediate problem. Anita now asked the difference between sex and rape, and Grandma replied, “Rape is what happens when the people aren’t married.” *Oh-oh* ... Look, I know where she was going here and why she simplified the explanation in this way, but how Anita perceived and stored the information led to a very basic conceptual misunderstanding of rape versus sex.

Later that year, Anita had an appointment for a gynecological check up at a large HMO. When Grandma saw that the assigned doctor was a black man like her rapist had been, she worried that the experience could be a traumatic ordeal. She therefore offered to accompany Anita into the examination room, but the girl refused and went in alone. When she emerged in cheerful spirits, Grandma asked her directly whether she had any concerns because the intimate examination was conducted by a doctor who was the same race as the man who had hurt her. Anita answered no, that it was Okay because she had seen his wedding ring and knew he was married. Oh-oh, again ... so, if another man—*heaven forbid*—assaults Anita and happens to be wearing a wedding ring, it's okay because that can't be rape?

This story illustrates the mind of the mentally young: linear, concrete, and limited in scope, just like that of a younger normal child. You cannot expect them to generalize information across similar situations without direct teaching, or to make what YOU think are rather obvious connections between item A and item B. And don't expect them to apply helping strategies that worked in one instance to a second, where it could be equally beneficial. If you directly teach them to do this, they will; but at some point down the line, the successful strategy will fade away unless there are repeated opportunities for practice and review. Welcome to the special education classroom.

**Appended Vignette**

Earlier in this chapter, I mentioned that prosecutors and police rarely contact experts to explain cognitive disabilities in perpetrators. These professionals therefore have less access to information regarding the identification and characteristics of affected individuals. The point of the following story is to illustrate how so-called "hidden disabilities" such as LD, ADD, and even ID, can be overlooked and/or misunderstood by untrained justice professionals. This common occurrence is what prompted the Office of Criminal Justice Planning to fund my three-year grant project to train police, probation, and attorneys in disability identification and accommodation. That training apparently did NOT include officers from this small police precinct that arrested a would-be burglar and placed him in one of their decrepit cells on a weekend hold. I later tested this defendant and can assure you that he had significant intellectual and adaptive deficits that interfered with function across <u>all</u> life domains. In fact, it was precisely these limited skills that led to the failed burglary and his immediate arrest. That occurred on a Friday evening as the precinct basically emptied out for the holiday weekend that followed. "Jerry" was therefore left alone and bored, with nothing but his dinner tray which contained a small yogurt and a plastic spoon.

Looking around the cell, Jerry noticed peeling paint on a side wall and went over to investigate further. He then saw that the underlying plaster was damp and crumbling, so he tried poking it with his spoon and was surprised when doing so created a small hole. By morning, Jerry's little excavation had punched an opening right through the crumbling wall into an empty hallway with a door marked "Exit" at the end of it. A little more digging and he was able to crawl through the opening and walk out the unalarmed door to freedom.

Jerry was easily recaptured, and the charges against him expanded to include absconding and evasion of arrest. Police paperwork that I reviewed as part of my assessment described the client as a criminally shrewd, devious mastermind rather than the pathetic bumbler that he actually was. By citing actual test data and observations, Jerry's lawyer was successful in getting the additional charges dropped. Although his "jail break" was rather embarrassing to the precinct, I like to think it resulted in additional funding to repair the decaying holding cells and thereby prevent a similar future event.

# PART THREE

# Other Issues

# CHAPTER FIFTEEN
## Ian, Severe Behavior Disorder

About fifteen years ago, I was asked by an out-of-state juvenile defense firm to assess a seventeen-year-old labeled with a Severe Behavior Disorder (SBD) by his school IEP (diagnostic and planning) team. This designation fell under a category now known as EBD (Emotional and Behavior Disorders), with only one to two percent of students qualifying nationwide. Youngsters diagnosed with EBD are primarily those who have trouble following directions, are oppositional, and can become aggressive toward others. They may also demonstrate an inability to build or maintain satisfactory interpersonal relationships with peers and teachers, and often display inappropriate behaviors or feelings under normal circumstances. Qualifying symptoms are not episodic, but persist over a long period of time and to such a marked degree that they adversely affect learning. Importantly, learning failure, if present, cannot be explained by intellectual, sensory, or health factors. With previous diagnoses of Conduct Disorder, Oppositional Defiant Disorder, and Depression, Ian fit this definition well. A possible Learning Disability was also suspected, though not verified, at the time of my assessment.

Regardless of how you label it, Ian was quite a handful in the classroom. He presented as a skinhead with explosive anger issues, especially toward women and minorities. He also had the remnants of a speech impediment (lisp) that had once received articulation therapy, and still popped up when he got emotional. This happened quite often.

The IEP team that verified SBD as Ian's qualifying disability agreed that he needed help to take better personal control as he matured. To do this, they came up with a plan that the youth would self-administer whenever he felt anger rising. The magic pill here was a ten minute "cool-out" option which allowed him to walk outside the classroom in order to head off an explosion, then calmly return to his desk. Teachers were notified that, per the IEP, he was allowed to use the cool-out option once a week in each of his classes. This plan was activated in the fall of the next school year, and everything seemed to be going well until a substitute teacher took over his computer class in early January.

How the problem began escapes me—maybe I never really knew. But what started out as a squabble with a classmate quickly escalated to angry posturing, so Ian alerted the teacher to his cool-out option and started for the classroom door. But the substitute prohibited him from leaving, saying that she wasn't made aware of any cool-out option. And she wasn't. No one had explained this procedure to her so she was left at a disadvantage. Ian didn't see it this way, however, and became furious—yelling, cursing, throwing papers—you get the idea. So, the alarmed substitute called in the Assistant Principal of Discipline (APD) to settle things down. The APD arrived in her own good time, allowing the emotional pot to simmer while she did so. She then verified that the cool-out option was indeed part of Ian's IEP, but this small victory did little to mollify the youth, who was by then pretty far gone. It was a very long day for everyone concerned. The result of the incident was that the IEP team reconvened mid-January to amend the plan so it couldn't fail again. The amended decision, with Ian there as a team participant, was to make and laminate an actual “cool-out card” for the youth to carry in his pocket and display to any teacher or substitute who was unaware of the option. Problem solved?

Well no, because only a few weeks later, another substitute took over the computer lab, and the identical scenario unfolded. Angered again by a classmate and preparing to leave the room, Ian displayed his card as per IEP instructions. However, this second substitute teacher refused to honor it saying, “That means nothing to me.” Ian went ballistic because it sure meant something to him. In fact, it appears that he had been clinging to the cool-out option for life support for some time while struggling in the “mainstream” of education. Indeed, the very purpose of the card was to ward off the violent outburst that was now unfolding. The APD was called in again to calm things down, but this time, Ian’s anger had escalated past the recovery level. He took aim at the APD (who had also attended his IEP meeting), calling her, among other things, a “bith” and backing her up against the wall. As Ian’s angry outburst escalated out of control, his face came close enough to hers that their noses briefly touched. Criminal charge: Assault. Ian was expelled from the school, though enrollment at an alternative program run by the district remained a possibility. But first, the assault charge needed to be dealt with in juvenile court.

### Trial, Part 1

At Ian’s initial trial, the defense made the court aware of his SBD diagnosis, current IEP provisions, and the breached cool-out procedure. The prosecution then put the APD on the witness stand to testify that she was so shaken by the violent incident that, after it was over, she had returned to her office, shut the door, sat down at her desk, and cried. This seemed to me an overreaction considering that the APD was already familiar with Ian, having had “previous incidences” as recent as two days prior to the time-out debacle. On this occasion, she was subjected to a string of profanity for asking the youth to utilize a designated walking route. A week before this, she had called a male security guard when this same youngster was involved in a classroom confrontation with a different substitute teacher. At that time, the APD had the opportunity to witness the security guard as he "verbally coaxed/directed" Ian away from the escalating situation, and was successful in "quieting him down" afterward. The APD therefore had prior first-hand experience with Ian's emotional outbursts, had witnessed effective de-escalation efforts, and had consulted with another employee regarding the best approach to take. She was also well aware of the time-out card option put into effect by his IEP team.

All of this background information had little to do with the fact that nose-to-nose contact had indeed occurred. Ian was therefore found guilty of simple assault, but the judge decided to take the case under advisement for a couple of weeks before determining sentencing. The youth was released pending this decision. That was when I entered the picture at the request of his attorney, the purpose being to assess the youth in order to provide the Court with as complete a picture of his situation as possible.

## Ian's Assessment

My assessment of Ian revealed academic skills that were fairly good considering how much time and effort he must spend to simply gain acceptable self controls. Here, his scores for reading and math ranged from sixth-to-eighth-grade levels, demonstrating a two-to-four-year lag for a beginning tenth grader. Standard scores for these subject areas were lower than optimal, but not so discrepant as to satisfy qualification criteria as Specific Learning Disabilities. Spelling alone scored far lower at the third grade level, earning a standard score of 68 which qualified for LD intervention. Why this had not been detected and targeted for remediation remains unknown; but it may have been more to do with Ian's troublesome behavior which had now escalated from malicious pranks such as flushing a student's hat down a toilet, to making racial slurs, pushing and kicking other students, and disrespecting teachers. By the end of his ninth-grade year, nineteen such incidents were documented in his file.

My report, therefore, included a sort of archaeological file dig which described this student's long history of SBD and past successful interventions. I also outlined the state's Education Code sections that mandated a district's obligation to carry out the provisions of the IEP as a legal document. I argued that the second breach of this written contract was the last straw that had fueled Ian's anger and frustration past the boiling point. Finally, I noted that a high school administrator charged with student discipline should be better prepared to deal with SBD kids enrolled on campus. This is especially true considering that she had attended the addendum IEP meeting as a district representative. Her job, as part of his team, then, became *sticking up for Ian* by updating the substitute teacher and publicly affirming the boy's cool-out option. I'll admit here that I was pretty steamed about the disgraceful way the school had handled this matter and pulled no punches in making this clear in my report.

### Trial, Part 2

When the judge resumed Ian's sentencing hearing a few weeks later, I was called to testify regarding the above findings. The judge then took some time to review my report in detail. The end result was that the guilty conviction rendered earlier was upheld, but Ian's sentence was entirely dismissed. He enrolled at the district-run alternative school the following Monday, which proved to be a far better "fit" for his particular behavioral issues. The incident also got the attention of a wonderful helping organization in that particular metropolitan area which unites social workers, educators, and other service professionals with the child and his or her parents to create a workable plan for future success. In essence, this organization conducts its own IEP meeting with the power to bring in volunteer and/or low cost services from outside the educational arena on an as-needed basis.

It is my hope that the APD learned a lesson here as well; namely, if you can't stand the heat ... well, it's more than that, really. Any school that has EBD or SED students on campus must prepare teachers and administrators to deal with the problems inherent in these disability conditions. That's why these kids are labeled "special" in the first place. And problems WILL arise because that's the nature of the beast. I'm reminded of a great line from the movie, *The Big Chill*, where one of the former college buddies, now a lawyer, discloses that she left the Public Defender's office because her clients just seemed "too guilty." Her old friend then remarks, "Well, who did you think your clients would be, Grumpy and Sneezy?"

This sums it up very well, I think: If you take a job in the kitchen, then prepare for heat. Likewise, if you are an AP of discipline, then prepare to discipline ALL of the students in your charge. This means that you will have to devise several levels of interventions, from slap-on-the-hand treatments for spitballs, to suspensions for a bit more serious campus violations, to really creative alternatives for handling the EBD crowd. The police should rarely *if ever* be called in to handle the behavioral infractions of a student with an IEP in place. That's because misbehavior that is a direct result of a child's disability profile is to be expected, planned for, and handled *internally*. Federal laws such as the IDEA, Section 504 of the Rehabilitation Act, and the Americans with Disabilities Act all address the issue of disability-based discrimination as something to avoid in public programs and proceedings. Accordingly, advocates for the disabled seek solutions that will ensure public safety while handling each client's unique needs in the least restrictive environment.

It is unfortunate that this educator was subjected to disrespectful treatment from a student, but handling it professionally was part of her job as disciplinarian on a campus that houses EBD classes. These programs do indeed contain difficult youngsters who live up to their designated labels. It is a fact of life that public schools must serve such students even though doing so can be quite challenging for all concerned.

# CHAPTER SIXTEEN
## Sean, Traumatic Brain Injury

Forty-year-old Sean was referred for assessment when his attorney discovered that he had suffered severe Traumatic Brain Injury (TBI) in a car accident when he was five years of age. Young Sean subsequently required intensive therapy to relearn speech and mobility skills, and spent many years in special education classes for students with one or more handicapping conditions. His attorney therefore sought an in-depth assessment in order to look more carefully at her client's current intellectual functioning; to examine any cognitive and/or language deficits which could interfere with the reception, processing, recall, and expression of information; and to determine whether he suffered from one or more specific learning or developmental disabilities as an adult. A total of almost six hours was devoted to Sean's direct assessment, which was conducted in a split (morning/afternoon) session in a secure jail setting.

### Case Background

I'll start by warning you that this was a simply horrific case which I might have rejected but for Sean's very dedicated and highly convincing Public Defender. It seems that her client had a long history of sex crimes against both children and adults which led to several previous adolescent and adult convictions. As such, deviant sexual behavior was seen as a "compulsion" that had not diminished while serving time in prison. This was not surprising considering that standard prisons have no specific programs in place to reeducate sex offenders in preparation for their eventual release. It is also why Washington, in 1990, and California, in 1995, along with many other states, enacted laws to prolong the confinement of some sex offenders beyond the end of their criminal sentences by means of indefinite "civil commitments" at state-run treatment facilities. In California, persons designated as "Sexually Violent Predators" or "SVPs" cannot be released from these civil commitments until they complete a five-phase treatment program (the so-called "Sexual Offender Treatment Program"), and are certified as "low risk" by two state-appointed doctors. But that was not the case when Sean was released from prison following what some considered a too-short sentence for his latest sexual assault.

Since Sean's time in prison had been merely punitive, no formal attempts were made to curb his long-established pattern of aberrant impulses. Instead, prison doctors prescribed several psychotropic medications which, according to Sean, merely "put me to sleep," and had little impact on altering his future behavior. Now released, he arrived back home by bus, but soon found he had nowhere to go. He hung around various parts of the city until locating an out-of-the-way transient park where a guy's actions remained his personal business.

It took some doing to piece together Sean's whereabouts during the two-year interim between his previous and next prison sentences, but I can offer a decent approximation. After hanging around his hometown a while, he went to Florida for a brief hiatus, and then returned to California where he and a male acquaintance rented a downtown apartment. It was here that Sean lured a young woman inside the apartment under the pretense of serving her a cold drink. He then bolted the door and proceeded to assault and rape her. She managed to save her own life by feigning enjoyment, and then concocted a story about needing to meet a friend at a party. Sean opted to drive her there, and gave her his address and phone number in case she would like to stay connected. This bizarre decision resulted in his return to state prison, this time, for a longer sentence.

During the time that Sean was between prison sentences (and therefore not in custody), two little boys were found dead in the same remote park that had been his most recent California hang-out. The boys had been tied up and left in a make-shift fort, and there was evidence of sexual molestation prior to their deaths. That crime occurred some years prior to an explosion of new advances in criminology. Thus, without proper technology to match any gatherable crime scene evidence to a suspect, the case went "cold" and remained unsolved for more than five years. During this time period, a lot of DNA evidence taken from bodies and rape kits was being stored for later analysis should it become possible through scientific advances. That was how, in a routine data scan, Sean's DNA popped up as a "match" to that found at the children's murder scene. This chance discovery was almost discarded as a one-in-a-million error because of Sean's current prison commitment ... *UNTIL* it was realized that he was indeed out of custody at the crucial time of the murders.

Now charged with the unsolved double murder, Sean was whisked back to his home city to prepare for the Guilt phase of his trial. A layer of complexity was added when he was concurrently charged with the rape and murder of a Florida prostitute when a similar DNA match identified him as the perpetrator. Since both trials could not go forward at the same time, Florida officials opted to wait their turn should the California case result in anything but a "guilty" verdict.

DNA evidence is quite compelling on its own, and doubly so when the suspect in question also has a proven compulsion that neatly explains the horrible treatment of his victims. As a result, Sean was found guilty and, as expected in any case where children are victimized, the District Attorney's Office opted to seek the death penalty in phase two of his trial. That was when I was brought into the case.

## Assessment

My assessment of Sean included a review of educational and medical records that supported his classification as a person with special needs. As the child of a military family, he had attended elementary schools in various locations across the country. Official records were sparse and incomplete, as were Sean's own recollections covering this time period. What he did recall was the car accident noted above, the lengthy period of hospitalization that followed, and having subsequent problems relearning speech, mobility, and virtually all academic material. Sean's self-reported learning problems were verified by available school records covering his second and third grade years while living in Georgia; and a later developmental history documented special education through much of his grade school experience.

When Sean entered junior high school in California, he was placed in an Educationally Handicapped (EH) class which catered to students with a variety of special needs. Teachers and counselors described him as emotionally troubled, and more than one of them suggested that this was due to an "abusive home environment." He was also seen as "hyperactive" and "prone to behavioral difficulties including angry outbursts." A medical evaluation conducted when Sean was thirteen indicated a "right sided [brain] lesion" with associated seizures that led to "psychotic episodes" that remained outside of his consciousness. Other records from a court-ordered treatment facility indicate periods of "blank staring" typically associated with a seizure disorder. The report from this facility diagnosed "significant memory impairment," as well as an Attention

Deficit Disorder in then fourteen-year-old Sean. Several psychostimulant medications (Ritalin, Cylert, and Dexedrine) prescribed to treat the latter condition seemed to ameliorate some of the explosive outbursts noted earlier. Having previewed his entire file, I was now ready to meet Sean in the flesh.

I was shown to a small interview room inside the downtown jail which had a single 8 x 10 inch window that looked out on an empty hallway. There was an intercom box on the wall in case I needed to call for assistance, but no noticeable guard activity in the immediate vicinity. The room remained locked throughout the test session. Sean entered in handcuffs which I requested be removed for testing purposes. Ankle manacles were then applied which attached Sean to his metal chair. None of this phased the client, who presented a calm, agreeable demeanor for the duration of the session. His established regimen of psychotropic medications was undoubtedly at least partially responsible for his compliant, though somewhat mechanical, behavior.

Sean was administered a battery of standardized tests which yielded a "low-average" IQ of 88 (range of 82 to 94), and academic skills that were adequate for community independence. Though no adaptive skill deficits in the *Practical Domain* were evident in domestic, vocational, and/or community environments, Sean's ongoing attention, memory, and information processing problems appeared to impact the *Conceptual* and *Social Domains*, and therefore suited the profile of one who has suffered a Traumatic Brain Injury. Because this condition, and his resulting seizure behavior, were documented to occur in childhood, both satisfied definitional criteria as Developmental Disabilities which, under California law, could qualify for services through the Regional Center system. It's a shame that this option, or a similar one had he been living out of state, was never explored, because services through this agency could have included sex education and counseling at Sean's developmental level.

## Trial(s)

The report of findings that I presented in testimony described Sean as one who had overcome the effects of his TBI well enough to develop a number of useful skills. He had achieved academic age-equivalents that varied between ages eleven and seventeen years, and vocabulary skills and language fundamentals between eight and fifteen years; but his information processing averaged below age nine. Ongoing attentional deviations were thought to be responsible for the sizable gaps that created this spiky profile. *Impulsivity* was a final difficulty related to both Sean's TBI and ADD that seemed to be at the root of his compulsion to act out sexually. My testimony was paired with that of a neurologist whose findings complemented my own. Our combined observations and test data painted a somewhat sympathetic picture which, in turn, resulted in a hung jury as to Sean's ultimate penalty. In other words, all twelve jurors had agreed that this brain-injured client was guilty of the terrible crimes; but questions lingered for some of them as to whether he could be considered fully responsible for them. Jurors who continued to wrestle with this question could not in good conscience render a death verdict.

The Assistant District Attorney reevaluated both the case and the public outrage surrounding it and subsequently opted for a retrial of the penalty phase. The neurologist and I were again called to testify and did so as before; but this time, the jury came back with a death verdict. Having come to know Sean quite well over the three trials, his attorney was utterly crushed. Considering the heinousness of his crimes and the fact that both victims were children, I was neither surprised nor crushed; in fact, I had been far more surprised when the jury "hung" the first time. Sean was returned to the state prison system, this time, as a condemned person on Death Row.

## Concluding Remarks

There's one more thing to consider in concluding this chapter, and that is the moratorium on the death penalty that currently exists across most of our nation and throughout the world. In fact, as of this writing, nineteen states plus the District of Columbia have enacted laws that completely abolish the death penalty. An additional seventeen states have imposed a moratorium on the death penalty due to pending legal challenges and/or a history of botched executions. Six of the remaining states where no formal hold is in place have not carried out the procedure for the past five years. The handful of states that remain have managed to conduct sixteen executions since 2010, placing our country's name on a very short list of those still adhering to this brutal policy. In this regard, the United Nations has called for a halt to the procedure in a resolution emphasizing that "... *the use of the death penalty undermines human dignity*" and that a moratorium would contribute *"to the enhancement and progressive development of human rights."*

Will the United States come out of the dark ages and eliminate the death penalty altogether? Only time, and the prevailing political winds, will tell. For now, we stand with Iran, Saudi Arabia, and a very few other countries which continue to believe that, much like corporal punishment will deter violence, killing will deter killing. Sean therefore marks off the days as he sits on California's only Death Row, now full to overflowing, at San Quentin Prison.

# CHAPTER SEVENTEEN

## Cory, Incompetent and Incapable

I am willing to bet that the vast majority of people have never even heard of Cory's unusual syndrome and have certainly never known anyone diagnosed with it. Well, I have. I met this youngster in the downtown office of his public defense attorney. He was thirteen years old and adorable. You see, kids with this syndrome are quite cute and diminutive in stature. They are also extremely friendly and loquacious, though intellectually disabled. With his IQ of 50, Cory fit this classic description perfectly. He also exhibited moderate to severe ADHD, and "verbal perseverations" (preoccupation with a few topics of interest) like those commonly demonstrated by autistic kids. Cory's verbal perseverations were mainly focused on body parts and emergency vehicles such as fire engines and ambulances. And he could be quite chatty about them.

As you may know, the lower the IQ, the younger one's mental age levels. Thus, although thirteen years of age *chronologically*, Cory's ability to think and reason resembled that of a four to five-year-old child. His attorney therefore raised questions that would address the client's capacity to commit a purposeful crime; namely, *Can someone like this understand that what he did was wrong?* Here's the story of Cory.

## Case Background

Because this youngster's parents were divorced, he lived with one of them and had visitation with the other. Cory liked to watch cartoons on television and would sit still for short time periods to do so. Next door to one of Cory's parents was a family with a four-year-old daughter whom the boy viewed as a potential friend. That's because, at age four, she was his "mental age mate," and the two shared common pastimes and interests. So, one day when bored with watching TV, Cory left the house to wander next door. Everyone in the neighborhood was already familiar with the friendly boy, so he was invited inside. Next thing you know, the neighbors observed Cory touching the little girl inappropriately (outside her clothing), and the police were called.

## Assessing Competence and Capacity

I must first say that this was the most adorable child I ever tested—though, admittedly, a handful due to his ADHD. Testing dragged on a bit as Cory was up and down to the window in his lawyer's office to look for emergency vehicles on the city streets below, and repeatedly wandered off-task talking about stomachs or livers, etc. But, we got the job done. Results verified moderate level intellectual disabilities, ADHD, and a mental age similar to that of the victim. Someone this young with all of these limitations can hardly be viewed as "competent to stand trial." This is because <u>trial competence</u> requires an understanding of the complex justice process, the ability to assist your lawyer in your own defense, and the self-control to behave properly in the courtroom. Because Cory had none of these abilities, I determined him to be "incompetent to stand trial."

The second issue in this case is a little more complex to explain, as well as to prove in a courtroom. This is the premise that Cory was also <u>incapable</u> of committing a planned and deliberate criminal offense. This determination was based on his four to five-year mental age scores across all of the various standardized tests, plus the fact that children at similar chronological ages have incomplete concepts of right versus wrong when it comes to touching behavior. In addition, Cory's ADHD made him highly impulsive, and his moderate intellectual disabilities limited the ability to plan, appreciate, or try to cover up the inappropriate touching behavior. His actions here were nothing more than curiosity spurred on by his persistent interest in body parts and fueled by impulsivity. Did he mean to hurt or embarrass the little girl? No. Was it still bad? Yes. Thus preventive alternatives were sought by his defense counsel.

A review of available records showed that the youngster's experience in terms of sex education was absolutely nil. Cory's teachers and parents thought of him as the very young child he was *mentally*, thus never brought up the subject. Knowing that he had a preoccupation with body parts should perhaps have been a tip-off that such behavior could occur, but his angelic face and charming naivety made such a thing hard to imagine. Cory himself expressed no guilt about what had happened, and did not try to negate, deny, or justify it. Thus, for all these reasons, his lawyer and I both portrayed him as *incapable* of committing a purposeful crime. Reviewing all available file and assessment data, the juvenile court agreed.

## Follow-up Education and Counseling

I have never before or since been involved in a case where *both* incompetence and incapacity were alleged by the defense. I think you will agree that Cory, being unique in so many ways, was an appropriate "first" in this department. As a result of the incident, he was put on six months' probation and ordered to attend counseling sessions with a male therapist who specialized in child sex offenders. The intention of therapy was to familiarize him with *"appropriate versus inappropriate" touching*. Over time, these sessions, and his sex education classes needed to add the *"public versus private"* element. This combination helps intellectually challenged individuals formulate a set of rules that *always* apply (in public and private), and to separate these from behaviors that will eventually be deemed permissible in private, though not necessarily appropriate in public. For example, holding hands is okay for people of all ages in public and private; while "making out" is reserved for private settings, and only by young adults who are __ years of age (parents: fill in the blank). Finally, forced touching is *never* okay in public OR private settings.

My favorite sex education program for use with intellectually disabled teens is the *Circles Stop Abuse* program cited in Chapter Eight. The Circles classroom display utilizes a wall-sized graphic composed of concentric circles in different colors to define close versus distant relationships. Each circle has its own slogan and hand signal to further drive home its point. So, the center (purple) circle represents your "private" self, the next (blue) "family" circle is for "close hugs," while the green "friend" circle is for "far away hugs," and so on. What I like most about the Circles program is the orange "wave" circle with its slogan, *"We never touch children; we only wave to them."* This is the sort of hard and fast lesson that even someone with a 50 IQ can memorize and say on cue. Whether someone at this reduced level will then act accordingly remains a case-by-case determination that will require continued supervision until the lesson is firmly encoded.

Ignoring sex education for disabled children, whether out of wishful thinking that they will never mature sexually, or out of fear that it will only prompt sexualized behavior, is an unwise thing to do. No matter the IQ, their bodies *will* mature and this will prompt all kinds of new thinking, behavior, and curiosity. Better to head off problems before they occur.

✧ ✧ ✧

Cory's story stands alone in some ways due to his unusual disorder and his combined incompetence/incapacity defense. The successful resolution of his case was aided by geography: he lived in a state that puts children first. Because of this, I separated it from the following chapter which addresses the plight of chronologically and mentally young defendants in a more general sense.

# CHAPTER EIGHTEEN
# Young and Mentally Young Offenders

This chapter continues and expands our previous discussion of how children—and adults who are their mental age-mates—fare in a justice system geared to prosecute typical adults who commit purposeful crimes. I'll begin with the story of the youngest "felon" ever referred to me for assessment. He was seven years old, and his crime was arson. Here is Jay's story.

## Jay, Age Seven

Jay was the youngest of four little boys, probably about a year apart. His mother had a chronic illness, thus was in and out of the hospital on a regular basis. His beleaguered father tried hard, but was sinking under the pressure of raising four boys virtually alone. Jay therefore got little attention at home and, with raging ADHD, had little attention of his own to devote in the classroom. So, his school district pulled a fast one on the family. Since ADHD did not then, in itself, qualify a child for special education, Jay was railroaded into the SED (Severe Emotional Disorder) program. This is an up-the-sleeve ace that school districts used to play where kids were a handful and parents remained unavailable. This described Jay's situation well. He WAS a handful in the kindergarten classroom—very bright and adorable, but into everything. So, they sent home assessment forms and IEP meeting invitations which, as expected, went unanswered. By law, an IEP meeting could be held without a parent present, as long as the district appointed an "advocate" to act on the family's behalf. That must be what happened here, because as he entered first grade, Jay found himself in the SED program. I still wonder what his overwrought parents must have thought the letters "SED" meant. Maybe "Special Education Determination?" I don't know, but they apparently signed off.

Even though the SED class was small (usually eight to twelve kids), Jay described being ignored by the teacher when I interviewed him for the Court. Don't forget, this was a child who needed an inordinate amount of attention, who thus became annoyed when the teacher was "always busy with the other kids." He was also being ignored at home by his busy father, ailing mother, and three older siblings who viewed him as sort of a pest. So, one day while walking to school, Jay found a book of matches lying on the ground. He put them in his pocket and hatched a plan: he would start a little fire in the class coatroom. *THAT* would grab his teacher's attention for sure. I must mention to you that the decision to seek this kind of negative attention is what my mentor professor called "the law of the soggy potato chip." Let me give you an adult example: You attend a party but arrive late. All that's left in the munchies bowl are soggy potato chips. You would like fresh ones, but if you sit there long enough, you'll eat the soggy ones. Well, it's the same for kids. If they can't have positive attention (which they would prefer), they'll take negative attention every time.

So that morning, while the teacher and aide were "busy" elsewhere, Jay entered the coatroom, pulled down an old paint smock, and lit it on fire. He showed me with hand gestures that he had planned his fire to be "this big" (about 1 x 1 foot) and "real smoky" so as to capture the teacher's attention. But that didn't exactly happen. As he said to me:

| | |
|---|---|
| Jay: | It's really the teacher's fault that the school caught on fire. |
| Me: | How do you figure that? |
| Jay: | She took the kids outside instead of taking care of MY FIRE! |

There you have the egocentric mind of the seven-year-old: *"The clouds follow me when I walk."* A child at this age level also believes that the plan or outcome he imagines is the ONLY way things can possibly turn out. So, the one-foot fire going out of control came as quite a surprise to Jay. Though it was extinguished without any widespread damage, it angered the administration considerably because the smoke filtered into and stunk up their offices. *So they called the police and filed charges of arson against the first grade SED (by their own definition) student?*

Jay was arrested and taken to the police station where he was read a standard adult version of the *Miranda* Rights. His verbal waiver of "Yes, Yes, and Yes" was quoted on the arrest report. Then, because of his young age, the standard warning was followed by California's *Gladys R.* interview per the following exchange:

| | |
|---|---|
| Officer: | Do you know the difference between right and wrong? |
| Jay: | Uh huh. |
| Officer: | Name something right to do. |
| Jay: | Go to school. |
| Officer: | Name something wrong to do. |
| Jay: | Fire. |
| Officer: | What happens if you light a fire? |
| Jay: | You get in trouble! |

Now satisfied that he knew the difference between right and wrong and had freely waived his *Miranda* rights, not one, but two officers proceeded to interrogate then six-year-old Jay without a lawyer, parent, or other advocate present. The Public Defender assigned to his case reviewed the entire incident in disbelief, thus called me to conduct a thorough assessment.

I met with Jay out of custody because, at such a young age, there was nowhere to *put* him, really. His father brought him to my office during the summer between his first and second grade years. He was bright and interesting, well-spoken and cute, but also had very high impulsivity and an ADHD score off the charts on my computer-based test. I then wrote a report explaining these outcomes along with a description of how the six to seven-year-old mind works. I went on to state that experimentation with matches was entirely explainable from a developmental perspective. In this regard, it is common for "preoperational" children (ages four to seven) to play with fire unless educated about potential risks and well supervised. They have only the most limited concept of the extensive damage and loss of life that can result when a fire spreads out of control. Jay therefore could neither envision the destructive outcome of his experiment, nor understand the lengthy legal entanglement that followed.

When his trial came up in November, I was called in to testify. I met Jay's family in the hallway outside the juvenile court. It was easy to spot them because of the four stair-step little boys and one haggard father. After greeting his dad, I walked up to Jay and crouched down to his eye level. "Hi Jay," I said, and noticed the inquisitive look on his face. "Don't you remember me? I'm the lady who tested you last summer."

Jay: You look different ... you look older.
Me: Thanks. You think it's the suit? (I was dressed more casually for testing)
Jay: No, it's your face and your hair.

So much for asking seven-year-olds anything that may require tact. They are just far too straightforward and truthful.

I will say that my heart sank a bit when I saw that the trial was to be held before the very well-known "hanging judge," but my fears were unfounded—it seems that even the strictest judge can appreciate cuteness when he sees it. I saw the twinkle in his eye as he looked at Jay, feet dangling from the chair, but not touching the courtroom floor. He listened to my testimony and then made his decision: six months on probation, and if you don't start any more fires, you're all done.

In closing Jay's story, let me once again issue this reminder to all school districts: If you determine that a child has a formal emotional or behavior disorder and they subsequently act out in expected fashion, *you should be ashamed of yourselves* for calling the police into it. You exist to *serve* such children, not to *prosecute* them. If you pay attention to their special needs and monitor proper behavior, such incidents will not occur in the first place.

## Treating Juveniles as Children

There's another take away from Jay's story; mainly, *size does matter*, and it matters a lot. Jay's young cognitive development matched his little body—we could all see this, even the prosecutor. But change the scenario to a slightly older child like Cory (Chapter Seventeen), or even a young adult like Gil (Chapter Six), with a similarly reduced mental age, and you will begin to understand the problems faced by other youthful defendants. In many of these situations, police, prosecutors, and even judges have trouble understanding the cognitive/body mismatch which is inherent in a typical disability profile. Happily, juvenile courts seem poised to listen and learn. That's a good thing, because this is the very reason these courts were invented in the first place: to deal with developmentally and cognitively young defendants in a fair and appropriate manner.

✧ ✧ ✧

But now let me introduce Donald, a sixteen-year-old youth with intellectual disabilities who had “mascot status” in a local Cripps gang. His case was handled in juvenile court as was appropriate for his age and offense. So far, so good. When found guilty as an accessory in a gang maneuver, he was placed at a county-run juvenile camp that *should* have been appropriate, but actually wasn't because Donald never quite understood the rules. One morning, at the urging of fellow wards who found his disability a source of amusement, the youth took an extra box of breakfast cereal because he was still hungry. As a result, he was placed in solitary confinement for a twenty-four-hour time period, crying and shivering in his underwear. Our intervention here resulted in the camp effecting a variable punishment schedule for lesser offenses like being hungry. We also seized the opportunity to educate staff about the *size* problem here—that Donald's mature height was at odds with his extreme mental immaturity. The bottom line is that, even though this youth's case was adjudicated in juvenile court, the punishment option presented challenges that remained above his cognitive capability.

✧ ✧ ✧

Then there's Jose, charged with a violent crime, whom I met at a county-run *adult* jail. Because Jose was seventeen and the crime was a serious one, he had been placed in the jail's growing “Juvy” unit. The sixteen- and seventeen-year-olds held here were dressed in red (as opposed to blue, orange, or white) jumpsuits for easy identification by staff. But this administrative decision posed an additional problem: the red outfits also provided useful information to predatory individuals, and thus endangered these teenagers' safety. Jose's parent therefore contacted several state advocacy groups which challenged the placement of juveniles inside adult jails. I believe that may have been the impetus to establish special handling units within the juvenile halls so that underage defendants charged with serious crimes could be housed with their chronological peers.

✧ ✧ ✧

## Youth in the Adult Justice System

This brings me to some final comments and statistics that illustrate the plight of children in a nationwide criminal justice system which has been anything but consistent in accommodating their developmental differences. Here, it is not uncommon for District Attorneys to insist on judging young defendants by their *actions* rather than their chronological or mental *ages*. One D.A. prosecuting a six-year-old for attempted murder (I'd love to know the back story on that one) commented that he didn't care whether a person was six or one-hundred and six ... "He was responsible for it. Period." Thinking like this illustrates the tenor of public sentiment in an age where children have done some uncharacteristic and rather shocking things. Fanned by the media, citizen outrage has led to a scrambling debate regarding how to best deal with children who break adult laws. That said, let me review a few foundational facts, many of which were provided by the Center for Prisoner Health and Human Rights:

- Approximately 2.1 million young people under the age of eighteen are arrested each year in the U.S., with girls the fastest-growing population in the juvenile system;

- 65% to 70% of these youth have one or more mental health disorders;

- An estimated 250,000 youth are tried, sentenced, or incarcerated as adults every year;

- About 10,000 youth are detained or incarcerated in adult jails or prisons on any given day;

- Three states allow twelve-year-olds to be tried as adults, while another fifteen set the minimum at age fourteen, and seventeen more have no minimum age at all;

- Due to the influx of thousands of children into the adult system, federal spending on prisons rose 30% while that spent on higher education dropped by 18%;

- By the year 2000, forty states had in some manner modified juvenile court confidentiality procedures to make these records more readily available.

There are even more dismal statistics to report once juveniles are sentenced to adult prisons. Whenever I talk about these data I think back to Danny in Chapter Four and wonder how he is doing. Well, as you might suspect, the statistics are chilling. Children placed in these facilities are five times more likely to be sexually assaulted and two times more likely to be beaten. Little wonder that the suicide rate for juveniles in adult prisons is fifty percent greater than for persons in the general prison population. Yes indeed, prison provides a real "education" in every sense of the word for the kids who are sent there. That's probably why those who live through the ordeal become more sophisticated criminals who are twenty-nine percent more likely to reoffend and come back through the revolving door.

I guess it all comes down to this question: At what age do we as a nation label a child as irredeemable? One state thought adult accountability should begin at age ten, but grudgingly settled for age twelve when advocacy agencies intervened. Considering the wealth of available data that describes the brain differences in children prior to age eighteen, I find this utterly shocking.

✧ ✧ ✧

So, let me close this chapter with some better news: Following the 2002 *Atkins* decision which vacated the death penalty for persons with intellectual disabilities, a 2010 Supreme Court decision ruled life without parole sentences for juveniles to be unconstitutional. Expert testimony in this case helped the Court to understand that even eighteen-year-olds are still undergoing brain development and therefore have a "diminished culpability, and a heightened capacity for change." A number of previous life sentences have since been altered to reflect that 2010 decision, potentially impacting up to three thousand incarcerated youth.

A wise judge in Los Angeles County liked to say that kids need three things to make it through life: 1) someone who cares about them, 2) something to do, and 3) something to look forward to. If more judges—not to mention parents, teachers, lawyers and police officers—realized and facilitated this, children who break the law might be offered the help they need to turn their lives around. Seattle's TeamChild program is a good example of money well spent to deter kids' future involvement in the justice system. Other programs such as Head Start and Big Brothers/Big Sisters represent our most powerful weapons in the war to deter juvenile crime. So are after-school sports clubs, summer camps, and peer-mentoring programs, all of which provide the "someone who cares" and "something to do" prescriptions offered by the judge. The bottom line is that we must recognize and acknowledge children's developmental differences, treat them accordingly when they get in trouble, and then fund programs that will hit the "restart" button before behavioral indiscretions spiral out of control. Not doing these things will only result in broken lives, high costs, and a tragic loss of human potential.

# CHAPTER NINETEEN
## Punishing Disabilities

This collection of disability-related case stories would not be complete without a discussion of how affected prisoners fare once sentenced to prison. The answer is: Not well. Having served as a principle expert witness in several class action lawsuits on behalf of disabled prisoners and parolees, my involvement in this matter is fairly extensive. The first of these lawsuits, which I'll refer to as the "A" case, was filed on behalf of prisoners with disabilities. The class included persons with Learning Disabilities, as well as vision, hearing, mobility and kidney impairments. Parts of the case were settled out of court, while others were tried in the 1990s, resulting in systemic changes for California prisoners with disabilities. Since then, civil law firms in several states have filed similar lawsuits based on evidence that disabled prisoners suffer inordinate hardships due to their inborn deficits. Let me further explain the foundation of these complaints.

### The "A" Case: Learning and other Disabilities in Prison

Most state prison systems are closed circuits with little outside infiltration or influence. Correctional Officers run the show, and if convicted individuals have a complaint—legitimate or otherwise—it may or may not be addressed. In fact, complaining can and often does mean that things will result in even worse treatment, so many of the inmates we interviewed for the lawsuit(s) had learned to simply shut up. But not Mr. A, for whom the class action lawsuit was named, whose disabilities prevented him from fully participating in various phases of prison life. Let me give you an example of a few of the unfair conditions that he and others like him encountered.

In the 1990s, California prisoners who were poor readers were excluded from vocational classes which opened the door to getting paid and/or higher level jobs within the prison. This means that people like Mr. A were prohibited entry based on nothing but their illiteracy. He and others like him also had difficulty reading personal and legal mail, not to mention directional signage around the various facilities. Finally, nonreaders encountered insurmountable barriers when presented with parole forms which coded Readability indices at college levels and beyond. Mr. A was experiencing many of these problems due to a Specific Learning Disability (SLD) that was diagnosed in early childhood. With help from his cellmate, he contacted a couple of civil law firms in the Bay Area, and the ball started rolling down hill.

These lawyers discovered that inmates with a variety of disabilities were being denied full access to prison or parole services in one way or another. Among these was George, the prisoner I mentioned briefly in Chapter Three. If you remember, he was prescribed heat-sensitive psych medications intended to calm ADD-related behaviors and, as a result, developed a seizure disorder when left all day in a hot exercise yard. But Gene's story goes a bit further. You see, this inmate could not read above a primer (second grade) level and therefore needed help filling out ducats requesting medical appointments. Annoyed with his continual requests following the onset of seizures, correctional officers refused to assist him more than once per month. As a result, he had to "save up" medical questions about seizure-related conditions that scared and worried him until the officers agreed to help him access his next doctor appointment.

In our interview, George shared a similar problem he had filling out the forms needed to get postage stamps. Accordingly, he had limited contact with the outside world. He also related one particularly frustrating experience that occurred in his living module. On the day in question, his cell door failed to open for breakfast, so he remained inside and hungry. At lunch, he stood at the door waiting, but once again, the door remained closed. Practically starving by now, he yelled out to the officer on duty and was gruffly told to, *"Read the sign!"* He couldn't do this, so he had to wait for another prisoner to return from lunch and clue him in. The sign said that, on this particular day (only), prisoners who wanted their doors opened for release to the mess hall had to turn on their cell lights. George hadn't followed these instructions, so he was forced to miss two consecutive meals without a verbal warning or explanation.

We discovered many similar breaches of logic, compassion, and common sense while working on this, and several subsequent lawsuits. In this regard, I interviewed an illiterate inmate who could not read the prison's directional signs; thus, he simply followed others around in hopes that they were going to his desired destination. Deaf people at this same prison reported a troublesome practice which I can only assume was a periodic drill of some kind, instituted by the administration. Here, officers would yell "down" in the busy exercise yard, and anyone who failed to immediately fall to the ground was shot with rubber bullets. As an aside, "rubber bullets" can and do cause severe injuries and even death if they strike key areas of the body. Since there were so many deaf people housed at this prison who were not "getting down," an administrative solution was devised: they put day-glow orange vests on the deaf prisoners to avoid shooting them. Perfect. Now all deaf people are easily identified by everyone, including predator inmates. What happened to a person's right to privacy?

## The "A" case: Learning and Other Disabilities in Parole Proceedings

Another person who stood out in this lawsuit was deaf and therefore required sign language interpretation for all parole hearings and procedures. Despite the Americans with Disabilities Act of 1990, the track record for the provision of interpreters in both the prison and parole systems was hit and miss. Apparently, some individuals working in the state correctional system did not believe the ADA applied to convicted felons. In other words, inmates had ceased being human beings once they were incarcerated. Mr. X, the deaf prisoner, was brought to federal court to testify in the "A" case regarding instances of unfair treatment caused by the denial of interpreters. The courtroom exchange between this prisoner and the state's attorney included discussion of a previous accommodation provided to him at a parole hearing. What followed clearly demonstrated that the officials in charge had little understanding of what sign language actually entailed, that it requires use of both hands, and that finger spelling with one hand is no substitute. The judge's post-trial written summary described the exchange well. Here, Mr. X stated that, even though a sign language interpreter was provided for his hearing, he was unable to communicate effectively with either his lawyer or the Parole Commissioner. That's because both his wrists were handcuffed at the waist during a brief pre-hearing meeting with his lawyer. For the hearing itself, one hand was freed, but the partial shackling prevented effective signage, and he had to resort to merely finger spelling a few words. Due to the communication hassle that followed, Mr. X decided that contesting the charge(s) against him would be futile, so he instead accepted a nine-month period of incarceration.

Unbelievable, right? What happened to common decency?

Many, if not most, illiterate parolees whom I interviewed or observed opted to "take the deal" offered to them at "parole revocation" (return to prison) hearings rather than to admit they could neither read the allegations, nor find and contact witnesses who might disprove them. The usual procedure was for the Hearing Officer to simply hand the parolee a stack of forms and tell him to "read these over," then make his plea(s). My observations of parolees who I knew to be illiterate and therefore unable to read the forms were two-fold: either they would pretend to be perusing the forms and quickly hand them back, saying "Okay" or, they would take so long struggling to decipher the forms that the Hearing Officer would get impatient and stop them from continuing. Comments like, "Aren't you finished *yet*?" heightened the parolees' embarrassment in this latter instance. Either way, justice was being derailed right before our eyes.

Finally, a number of prisoners in wheelchairs told us that they were made to crawl up several stairs to parole proceedings that could have been held in accessible rooms. These individuals also complained that they were being held to the "two-minute shower" rule despite special needs that required more time for adequate hygiene.

Suffice to say that the federal judge presiding over the "A" case didn't wait to write her opinion in a formal document, but issued a bench decree in favor of the plaintiffs. The prisons were then barred from wreaking inordinate hardships on disabled prisoners by continuing any practices that denied them access to programs and services. Likewise, the parole system was ordered to rewrite all of their forms at lower literacy levels, so they hired me to do just this for almost seventy forms currently in use. Parole was further ordered to provide attorneys to assist disabled parolees in hearings where new charges were brought against them. After two additional lawsuits were brought on behalf of people who were illiterate but lacked a formal disability classification, this provision was eventually extended to *all* parolees who asked for legal help before signing their lives away.

## The "C" Case: Intellectual Disabilities in Prison

A second class action lawsuit concurrently filed with the "A" case involved similar complaints on behalf of prisoners with "mental retardation" (now termed Intellectual Disabilities or, ID). The two cases were compiled simultaneously; thus, my intense involvement with the "A" case prevented similar work on the original "C" case. The outcome of that federal trial was that California prisons were ordered to create and administer a comprehensive program that would assist prisoners with ID in every phase of prison life. This led to a 2002 "Remedial Plan" covering modifications to be instituted in the housing units, vocational programs, medical facilities, schools, canteens (prison stores), and virtually all other prison venues.

The "C Remedial Plan" became an official document more than fifteen years ago. To better facilitate it, eight prisons were made "disability friendly," and many or most of the deaf, wheelchair-bound, and blind population were transferred to these sites. Importantly, these so-called "designated" prisons included a population of typical (nondisabled) individuals, along with inmates with moderate to severe Intellectual Disabilities, labeled DD2 and DD3 during the intake process. Others with similar DD classifications were identified when reports like mine followed them into the Reception Centers. Prisoners considered to have "mild" intellectual disabilities were labeled "DD1" and scattered between the designated and standard prisons. How their placements were determined still remains a mystery to me; but knowing the sheer numbers with potential qualification explains the need to house some of the higher functioning DD1s in standard prison locations. The "C Plan" stated that the eight designated prisons would provide specially-trained officers to assist DD prisoners with a whole host of daily living activities. The list of assisted activities included hygiene routines, using the canteen (prison store), securing and following through with medical appointments, reading signs and documents, and attending classes, jobs, and other appointments. On paper, it sounded pretty good.

## Monitoring Dispute

The legal team involved in the original lawsuits continued to monitor the administration of the "C Plan" at the designated prisons for several years. Things seemed to be moving along toward one day becoming an adequate program which would humanely house these disabled inmates. I feel obligated to state here that California has been a leader in this regard. Indeed, if prison conditions in *this* state are even marginally substandard, I can only imagine how ghastly they are in less progressive states. Nevertheless, our constant monitoring of the "C Plan" proved necessary for at least the first ten years of its implementation. But then, suddenly, in 2009, the state decided they had had enough outside monitoring. So, they brought a termination motion in federal court, stating they were adhering to the "C Plan," and that the system was therefore "fixed." They further argued that the case should be dismissed, and all court involvement should end, including monitoring by plaintiffs' counsel and experts.

## Status Declarations

Now put on the defensive, the civil law firm handling the "A" and "C" lawsuits hired an independent consultant/expert to visit seven designated prisons in order to interview DD2 and DD3 individuals. The point of these visits was to determine whether the "C Plan" had magically taken care of their issues and problems. I was also rehired to write a declaration explaining what we *would expect* to find if the prison system *WAS NOT* adequately caring for these disabled prisoners. Without any consultation between myself and Dr. L, the independent expert, our reports matched almost identically. In other words, my hypothetical expectations that X, Y, and Z would happen if the prisons were not meeting the needs of disabled individuals, perfectly paralleled the other expert's report which found that X, Y and Z *were indeed* happening per his interviews with over one hundred fifty DD prisoners.

The experiences that DD2 and DD3 inmates shared with Dr. L were detailed in his declaration which verified egregious breeches of human compassion, neglect bordering on abuse, and outright mean treatment by certain correctional officers named repeatedly by the inmates. One particular "bad" officer was identified by nine prisoners for what appeared to be purposeful, spiteful behavior. He and several others were described by DD prisoners as threatening and belittling them, as well as "throwing them up against the wall" on occasion. What in the world were people like this doing at prisons designated for disabled, and therefore needy, individuals? In fact, why would anyone with such a vicious attitude be hired at *ANY* prison?

These allegations of abuse were brought up by the state's attorney in the federal trial that followed. During my testimony in the matter, this lawyer pressed me about this particular officer's identification by inmates with known cognitive limitations, alleging that they often "made things up" and were therefore untrustworthy. My response to this accusation was that these multiple prisoners, with no opportunity for collusion, could not have hallucinated the officer's abuses. He was indeed a belligerent individual who needed immediate reassignment or outright firing. DD2 and DD3 inmates also named a few "good" staff members who deserve a lot of credit for sticking up for them in that punitive climate. The fact that many of these heroes were women and, in some cases, Hispanics, came as no surprise to me, in that my doctoral dissertation found the same thing: female and Hispanic high school students displayed more favorable attitudes and better treatment of their disabled classmates.

### Summary of Expected and Unexpected Problems for DD Prisoners

At this point, let me present a brief summary of difficulties we *expected* to find if DD inmates were being denied appropriate supports, along with Dr. L's *actual* findings. I want to stress that the complaints and abuses described here represent only a fraction of those reported by the hundred fifty-two male prisoners who were interviewed. Some of them expressed fear in coming forward, and thus were assured anonymity through the use of research numbers rather than their names or prison ID numbers. Here's some of what they reported.

We DID expect the men to report problems using the canteen (prison store) if forced to do so without assistance by correctional staff. This was because their poor math and reading skills could lead to errors filling out requisition forms and paying for goods. But we DID NOT expect to hear so many reports that they were robbed of all their purchases by nondisabled prisoners while returning to their cells without a staff escort. Many others reported theft of personal belongings from their cells or lockers even though the Department of Corrections had engraved their inmate numbers on property such as radios and CD players that should have secured their easy return. To return these items to their proper owners, officers would have to initiate a search that would take some time. Accordingly, the typical response to complaints of theft was that they were "too busy" to look into it. As a result, one disabled prisoner lost an entire care package of goods his mother had just sent, including new tennis shoes and a large assortment of food and toiletries. Another came back from taking a shower to find that his new television had been stolen. No attempts at recovery were undertaken.

An inability to read led to a number of related problems among the prisoners who were interviewed. Here, we DID expect those with disabilities to have problems reading their personal and legal mail—but DID NOT expect them to lose all control over this sensitive information by having to ask sometimes untrustworthy others to read it aloud to them. In these and other instances where reading help was needed, DD inmates were forced to "pay" by trading soup packets or portions of their meals. The price reported by one such individual was two to three soup or coffee packets to write a letter, and one or two more to have a letter read to him. We also DID expect to find prisoners who could not fill out proper forms to make medical or dental appointments; but DID NOT expect to find so many who let all such appointments go for the duration of their sentences because no help was available. Some of these men had medical and/or dental conditions that went untreated, and one was forced to rely on his cellmate's eyeglasses which he said were "a little blurry."

Most illiterate prisoners had no knowledge that numerous forms existed and were available to them to lodge formal complaints; neither could they complete these high-level forms if they tried. One particular individual had learned of a form which he could use to appeal unfair treatment, but was told by a staff member that if he made any mistakes filling it out, he would lose all of his property. Another disabled prisoner visited the prison library to ask for help filing a claim, only to be told by the library assistant that she was not allowed to help with complaints against the state.

We DID expect, and found, instances where DD prisoners committed a number of rules violations, many of which were the result of failing to understand proper behavior in the first place. Others were linked to their inability to read posted rules. One man said he received several disciplinary write-ups for "forgetting stuff and not locking up." A number of those interviewed by Dr. L were seen while placed in the segregated (Ad-Seg) disciplinary unit. One of these men reported being held in Ad-Seg for a month but did not know why or how much longer he would have to stay there.

One particularly consistent finding by the independent expert was how out-of-the-loop these prisoners were when it came to socialization, friendships, and contact with the outside world. Some had avoided writing letters due to illiteracy; while others, like George, could not fill out the necessary forms to access stamps. Accordingly, two DD prisoners reported that they had only recently found out that close relatives had died, but that no one had informed them about the deaths. They were only now experiencing grief for losses that had occurred one to two years prior.

Finally, we DID, sadly, expect to hear of random instances of physical abuse inside the designated prisons; but we were not prepared for the volume of such complaints from DD inmates so easily targeted by others. These men reported physical, sexual and verbal abuse, along with exploitation and harassment in a system that remained indifferent to their needs. A number of inmates reported being afraid to take a shower for fear of being assaulted by others. The dirty and unkempt appearance of these inmates highlighted the fact that they were neither monitored to maintain personal safety, nor prompted by guards to shower or change clothes regularly. All in all, our combined reports presented a scathing account of failure that proved the need for continued external monitoring of the "C Plan."

**Summary**

In closing this chapter, let me summarize the "A" and "C" lawsuits in this manner: People are still people no matter what they've done, and do not surrender their human dignity just because they are serving time in prison. The Americans with Disabilities Act still applies to the incarcerated population, as does Section 504 of the Rehabilitation Act. The difficulties of prison life are substantial to be sure—no one ever said it would be a garden party—but these hardships *cannot be permitted to bear more heavily on disabled than nondisabled prisoners*. Continuing the unfair practices and conditions described by this plaintiff class of individuals amounts to selective discrimination based on their disabilities. The ultimate purpose of these and other disability rights lawsuits is to insure that *fundamental fairness* extends to all, even inside closed and previously impermeable environments. Shedding light on the discriminatory practices that festered there was the only way to change them. The "A" and "C" lawsuits undertook this process on behalf of prisoners and parolees with a variety of disabilities and, in so doing, upgraded our prison system to one of the best in the nation.

# CHAPTER TWENTY
## My Video(less) Lesson Plan

After twenty-five years assessing people in serious trouble, it occurred to me that teenagers could really use a "lesson" to avoid similar entanglements with the justice system. I had a grand idea that involved obtaining a federal grant to make a video and pairing it with lesson plans, case studies, and other teaching materials for use in high school classrooms. I even chose three young men who would "star" in my video because they were not only charismatic, but also presented sadly convincing arguments for caution in social situations that could lead to trouble. But, here is the rub: prisons and jails rarely *if ever* allow videotaping inside any portion of the facility, and these three men won't see the light of day any time soon. You see, although all three were sentenced to life <u>with</u> the possibility of parole, those hearings were not scheduled to even begin to take place for about twenty years.

Even though I have written off the video lesson as a virtual impossibility, I still think about my three would-be "stars" and how appealing they would be to other young people. One was twenty-year-old Tom, who led off the Ground Rules chapter of this book with his insightful comment, "It only takes a second."

The second was Mike, a high school senior in California's Central Valley. The third was Jason, a local boy who was also a senior in high school at the time he was arrested. Together, they presented the biggest waste of human potential ever assembled in my mind. All were nice looking boys from good families in decent neighborhoods, who had made it past the sometimes stormy adolescent period and almost found clear paths to adulthood. One was on his school's wrestling team, another was college bound, and the third was juggling junior college with a part-time job. All of their dreams and plans were dashed on the fateful nights when those crucial "one second" moments occurred. As I write this today, years after meeting each one of these youths, I will admit to feeling a great deal of emotion. Let me introduce each one to you now.

### Tom, Age Twenty

Tom's tragic story was fully detailed in a long magazine article just after he and his four teenaged friends were sentenced. That article got national attention due to the word "lynching" in the title. The author was *not* referring to the victim, a local drug pusher, but to his five young customers who received maximum sentences from a judge with an ax to grind. Only one of these boys committed the actual murder with a concealed weapon that the others didn't know about; but, the fact that they were merely <u>there</u> led to four additional life sentences. This common occurrence—guilt by association—is something that should be emblazoned on a poster and plastered in every teenager's bedroom: If you are simply THERE when a crime is committed, you are also considered "guilty" and may have to pay for it with several years of your life.

Tom's lesson is two-fold.

First, know who you are accompanying and where they plan to go. Find out what these friends and/or acquaintances expect to do once they get there. Be curious. Ask questions, and don't worry about looking like a nerd for doing it. Learn whether anyone has a gripe to settle, an anger problem, and/or is carrying a weapon—ANY weapon, including a two-inch pen knife.

The second lesson concerns that crucial moment when a person can still take the opportunity to run away from an escalating situation. If things suddenly heat up, get away as fast and far as you can, and then call someone to come and pick you up. Parents should make an agreement with their teenaged kids along these lines. Tell them it's okay to call *at any hour* if they are in trouble, and that you will come and get them—no question asked. Or, parents can go ahead and ask the questions, as long as they also reward the fast thinking and sheer guts it took for their teenager to put some distance between him or herself and the unfolding crime. If this isn't the sort of information you want your parent to know, then make a similar arrangement with someone else or, put Uber or Lyft on speed-dial. Just do it.

### Mike, Age Seventeen

Mike was a teenager with a Specific Learning Disability (*dyslexia*) that targeted reading. He was receiving partial-day help through the Resource Specialist Program at his high school, and was trying like heck to keep this fact from his peers. Mike made the wrestling team in the fall of his senior year and, several weeks into the season, was invited to join a group of teammates one Friday night. The loose plan involved a joyride out into a remote area of the county, then maybe stopping for burgers, and crashing at someone's house. Since Mike's shyness and need to mask his dyslexia had thus far distanced him from most social activities, he was excited to finally have friends. So he joined six other wrestlers for what he thought would be a fun night. Fitting seven teenagers inside one car is difficult, so two of them were actually riding inside the trunk as they wound their way out of town. Mike fell asleep in the back seat, only to be awakened by shots firing. To his horror, the gunfire seemed to be coming from the driver of the very car in which he was sleeping. Result: one dead drug dealer and a speeding car full of wrestlers making a clumsy getaway.

All seven of the kids in that car were arrested and taken to the nearest juvenile hall. The five boys riding inside the body of the car, including Mike, were charged with murder, while the two in the trunk received a lesser charge. By the time I got involved in the case, the shooter/driver and three other passengers had received life sentences. My assessment detailing Mike's dyslexia was accompanied by a discussion of his social isolation and need for friends. The court apparently took this to heart, and therefore awarded Mike the only life sentence that carried the possibility of parole after a prescribed period of time. Needless to say, this hit the local high school really hard, and the wrestling season was decimated.

In terms of the lessons in Mike's story, I would refer you to the same ones listed for Tom, above: know who you're going out with; check the details; learn whether there's any back story prompting the proposed outing; and get away if there's trouble. When I think of that speeding car leaving the wilderness area, I like to envision a different ending, where all of the car doors and the trunk spring open, and six boys jump to safety. The driver/shooter is then left alone to pay for his crime. Maybe a few broken bones might have resulted, but recovering from a fractured arm is far preferable to spending a lifetime in prison.

There was one more detail in Mike's story that is particularly pertinent for teenagers to consider, and that was his agreement to talk to the arresting officers without an attorney or parent present. NEVER ... DO ... THIS. At age seventeen, Mike had the right, not only to counsel, but to have a parent brought into the interrogation room for moral support and assistance. Teens need to know that, even for minor charges, they should <u>always</u> ask for an attorney and keep asking until one is provided. Take a look at Appendix B, and you will see why. Here, Allen, Charles, and Damon all agreed to speak without counsel present, and look how they turned out! The decision to speak without a lawyer is usually driven by a couple of false assumptions: First is the immature notion that the police are "your friends" and helpful community heroes, and thus are to be trusted. No, they're not. Not when you are suspected of a crime. Second is an equally naive belief that cooperating with and/or helping the police will get them to reduce your charge and intervene on your behalf at trial. It probably won't. Not unless you have confidential information to offer them that will help catch a major offender, and a "deal" is struck. Your lawyer would need to be present for this to happen—don't try it on your own.

### Jason, Age Eighteen

For me, this is probably the saddest of thee three stories, primarily because the boy in question had such a promising future. I should begin by stating that Jason was popular at his school and in the community at large. He was college-bound in only a few months and was attending a party with other seniors to celebrate their impending launch into the future. When I received Jason's file from the public defender handling his case, it contained twenty-one letters of support from clergy, teachers, employers, family, and neighbors, all of whom verified his good character and begged for leniency. This is what happened.

Jason was at a house party having a good time when a past graduate I'll call the "intruder" came in, drunk, with a female friend. The intruder began by getting loud and vulgar and then escalated to physically pushing and shoving some of the kids around. Warning comments had no impact, and the intruder continued to ruin the party by being a general annoyance. But when he turned his belligerence on the female who came in with him, Jason had had enough. He intervened by getting in the intruder's face, and a fight broke out. Jason was smaller than his opponent and seemed to be taking more punches. Maybe that's when and why someone threw a knife into the fracas. I can only guess that two hands reached for it at the same time, and Jason won. The stab wound that resulted shouldn't have killed the intruder, but enough time was wasted getting him help that it did. Jason's sentence was life in prison with the possibility of parole. I only hope that the twenty-one people who wrote letters of support will be at his hearing when that day comes.

The lessons here are fairly obvious: Never start a fight with a drunk and don't react by grabbing a weapon if you do. Should a weapon suddenly become available, kick it aside so that nobody will be tempted to use it. But the easiest fix would take place before the situation escalates to this point, and that is to call the police to take the intruder away. Yes, it might shorten your party by a few hours, but if you're smart about it, no one will end up in jail.

### One More Story

I'll start by stating that I don't know the two boys in this story. It was passed along to me by an attorney friend who assisted in their appeal case. It occurred about twenty years ago in a state I have never worked in. Here's what happened.

Two eighteen-year-old boys hatched a plan one boring afternoon. They decided to shoplift a bottle from a small liquor store located in a local strip mall. They drove to the mall and parked their car in full view of anyone who happened to be shopping in an adjacent store. They then entered the liquor store and were surprised—no, *delighted*—to find it totally empty! So, with no shopkeeper in sight, they each took a bottle and left the store laughing. What they didn't know was that, twenty minutes earlier, the shopkeeper had been robbed and killed, and that his body was lying on the floor behind the cash register counter. The boys were easily identified by shoppers, subsequently charged with the murder, and found guilty. They spent nine years in prison before the real perpetrator was discovered. Yes, nine years of their young lives were lost due to a really stupid decision. Keep that in mind, along with Dr.

Cunningham's *"One boy is a boy ..."* slogan (see Chapter One), and remember how easy it is to lose your grounding when accompanied by peers. Don't let your friends talk you into a dumb stunt that will almost certainly lead to trouble.

✧ ✧ ✧

## Discussion Questions

I want to conclude this chapter by suggesting a number of discussion questions for teenagers. These incorporate the cases above and in previous chapters, plus a few that I have not included in this book. All of them are true. I would propose that parents and teachers facilitate open-ended discussions so that honest dialog can take place.

<u>Situation #1: Tom and Mike, Above</u>

Tom and Mike fell into similar situations where they were out with friends when plans were made that led to trouble. There was a point in each of these stories when there was still time to back out. Neither boy did this, but instead relied on their friends to make key decisions for them *("... and three boys—that's no boy at all.")* In each case, the group plan was orchestrated by one volatile member with an ax to grind.

<u>Questions</u>:

1. What might be some signs that a proposed group plan could lead to trouble?
2. How can you extricate yourself from a potentially dangerous group decision?
3. Do you have an obligation to yourself and/or the others to redirect the plan to a less risky one? What's the best way to do this?

✧ ✧ ✧

Situation #2: John, Chapter Five

John was attempting to implement the burglary scheme that had been used by an acquaintance but went off track with a disastrous result. In his chapter, I mentioned a few self-monitoring strategies that can help confused or impulsive young people to ***S****top*, ***T****hink*, ***A****ct*, and ***R****eview* their plans once underway. Perhaps if John had used this so-called "STAR" method, his only crime would have been burglary.

Questions:

1. Could memorizing a self-monitoring strategy help someone like John stay on track?
2. Once arrested, John mistakenly thought he could extricate himself by outwitting the police with a succession of false stories. When should he have realized he was totally out of his league? What should have been his next move?
3. It might be fun to make up your own acronym to prompt the request for a lawyer. One suggestion revises STAR to: **S**top, **T**hink, **A**sk, and **R**epeat the request. Any others?

✧ ✧ ✧

Situation #3: Gil, Chapter Six

Gil was essentially lured to admit to a crime he didn't commit in order to impress a cute girl. He falls for her flattery and begins to paint an unrealistic self portrait as a street-smart gangbanger, when in fact, he was just an *in*secure security guard with a weight problem. In a subsequent conversation, an undercover gang leader scares and threatens Gil into further implicating himself as the shooter in the recent drive-by crime.

Questions:

1. At what point in his conversation(s) with the undercover female detective should Gil have realized he was being played? Why do you think he didn't?
2. A lawyer wouldn't have been much help to Gil in his conversation with the gang leader. This is a tough one, but can you think of any other way he could he have handled the "Green Light" threat without endangering *or* incriminating himself?

✧ ✧ ✧

Situation #4: Ian, Chapter Fifteen

Ian's explosive anger prompted his IEP team to assign a "cool out" card which entitled him to leave class, walk outside, defuse the anger, and return to his desk once calm. When two substitute teachers ignored the remedy, he spiraled out of control, eventually taking aim at the vice principal who was called in to handle the situation.

Questions:

1. How else could Ian and/or the vice principal have handled this episode?
2. What percentage of the blame for the assault should be assumed by the school district? Conversely, how much is Ian's fault? Does blame increase with age?

✧ ✧ ✧

Situation #5: Charles, [See Appendix B]

Charles knew he was entitled to a lawyer if arrested, but when actually immersed in the situation, waived this right away.

Here, he was easily fooled by police who offered partial truths about when and where he could access a lawyer. Confusion about the phrase, "an attorney will be appointed for you ..." eventually overwhelmed him. The youth therefore agreed to an unassisted interrogation that led police to file murder charges in what became a capital case.

Questions:

1. Should schools teach units about the legal rights of minors in an arrest process?
2. What other self-advocacy strategies should be discussed? Would it help if kids carried cards in their wallets that listed their legal rights and lawyer's phone number?

✧ ✧ ✧

Situation #6(a): Derrick

Derrick had just returned to his home after spending nine months in a juvenile detention facility. He was now eighteen, and no longer a minor. Derrick wasn't back for more than a week when a friend approached him saying, "You owe me money—you owe me a thousand dollars." The friend then laid out his plan to rob a nearby McDonald's in the late night hours when a single employee would be manning the location. He then proposed, "You take the gun and go in, and I'll be waiting right outside the door in my car with the motor running so we can make a quick get-away."

Questions:

1. How important is repaying a debt to a friend? Is it worth risking your own future? Was there another way for Derrick to repay it?

2. Is Derrick being used by his friend? If so, why doesn't he know it?

✧ ✧ ✧

Situation #6(b): Derrick – Extension

Derrick entered the McDonald's and found that his friend was right—the only person around was a single employee about his own age running the counter. He opened his coat to display the gun and told the clerk to hand over all the money. The terrified youth responded that the day's earnings were in the safe and he needed the approval of his manager to open it. Derrick tells him to, "Go call him up." The clerk was allowed to make two such phone calls before getting the manager's approval, the safe combination, and instructions to give Derrick the money, "real slow."

Questions:

1. When Derrick finally got the money and ran out the door, where do YOU think his friend was? Who do YOU think was waiting there instead?
2. If Derrick is offered a "deal" to give up his friend's name, should he do it?

✧ ✧ ✧

Situation #7: Joe

Joe was a nonreader with severe dyslexia who was arrested on a murder charge. Police put a written *Miranda* warning and a longer Waiver of Rights form in front of him which he pretended to read. They then told him to initial every sub-statement. The result was a full page waiver where the small blanks next to the statements each contained the large handwritten notation: *JF, JF, JF* ...

Questions:

1. Is there ever an instance where it would be appropriate to sign a document you cannot read and fully comprehend?
2. If a high level, and therefore hard to understand, document is put before you, what should your response be?
3. If the serving party (e.g., police) insists that you *must* sign it, what recourse do you have?

✧ ✧ ✧

All parents should conduct a discussion along these lines, not only with their sons, but also their daughters. Remember, girls currently represent the fastest growing population in the juvenile justice system. Set up some hard and fast ground rules that the family can brainstorm together. Make agreements about particular friends and situations to avoid. Role-play one or more strategies teens can use to extricate themselves if trouble should arise.

And remember Tom's warning: It only takes a second!

# CONCLUDING REMARKS
## "Out Like Michael Jordan"

I made a decision years ago that I wouldn't wait to retire until I got old and dotty because this work was too important to risk it; instead, I would go out like Michael Jordan, at the top of my game. I hope Michael doesn't mind being my inspiration and muse in this regard, but he provided the perfect model for my similar path as an "expert" in a different field.

For a long time, my phone would ring with lawyers lamenting my retirement and, in some cases, begging me to take "just one more" before leaving. I refused because I had seen how women are treated as they age, gracefully or otherwise. Strange men stop calling you "Babe" or "Hon" and instead morph to "Ma'am" or, the ultimate insult, "Dear." Worse yet, your years of accumulated experience and wisdom are now viewed as somewhat dated and maybe not quite so relevant. So, the bottom line is, I didn't want to ever go there.

I will admit that my retirement left a big hole in the discipline that now needs filling, but I'll get to that in a minute. Sure, there are dozens if not hundreds of "panel psychs" available to conduct mental status and competency evaluations. Many of these individuals will tell lawyers they are thoroughly familiar with the cognitive disorders that were my specialty. Unfortunately, as a general rule, they are not, and simply want the work.

My Ph.D. coursework consisted of in-depth study of learning, cognition, information processing, attention, and language, with only the most peripheral focus on the mental and emotional disorders found in psychology manuals. Although my degree is in "Educational Psychology," I am an *educator*, not a psychologist. And I never said I was one. Lawyers on both sides of the aisle assumed it all the time, but I corrected them when they did. If I had pretended to have expertise as a clinical psychologist, I would have been sued out of existence by the APA. But, for some reason, the same does not appear to apply in the reverse: psychologists feigning educational expertise will not have to face an irate PTA.

My expertise therefore pertained to the role that a client's reduced cognitive skills may have played during the commission of his crime. I was also concerned with his comprehension of the *Miranda* warning and the arrest process in general, his ability to participate knowingly as a self-advocate in the trial process, and how his deficit pattern would impact so-called "rehabilitation" if remanded to prison.

In some cases I was called upon to verify his competence to stand trial and make a case for *diversion* in lieu of prison for certain low-functioning clients. But to do any of these things, I needed to compile a complete skills profile from test data that took hours to collect, and create a lengthy (usually, 16–22 or more page) report which served to educate the lawyers from both sides, along with the judge and the jury.

I had a number of cases where information from a given prisoner assessment raised questions that impacted the Guilt phase of his trial. Did he really do it, or was he simply prompted to confess in order to please the police? Could someone functioning at this reduced level of competence be held fully accountable for his actions? Was he duped into, or otherwise directed to carry out a crime by a more competent peer? Did he have the mental maturity to even understand that what he did was actually wrong? My findings could also explain certain bumbling errors that led to unintended consequences. Unfortunately, a person's ability to understand and appreciate all possible consequences of his actions usually carries little weight in the courtroom. Indeed, the law is more concerned with the *outcome* of an action—if you intended to act at all and things go disastrously wrong, the consequences are on you. So, my client who knocked an old lady down when he only meant to snatch her purse found himself indicted for murder when she died of a related blood clot two months later. His *intention* was to commit a fairly minor crime, but he now faced trial on a far more serious charge.

Information pertaining to a client's cognitive disabilities can also be used in Penalty phase trials, the intention being to present as full a picture as possible to the jury that will decide his fate. They need to know just who is sitting before them in order to insure fundamental fairness all the way around. Does it matter that he thinks in much the same manner as a five to seven-year-old child? Is an IQ that falls below ninety-seven percent of his age-mates important to know? Should mercy be shown to someone who spent his school years fearful and embarrassed, worrying every day that his deficits would be put on display for ridicule by his peers? Should brain-based issues related to heredity, prior head trauma, or inborn impulsivity be considered?

So, yes, the penalty should fit the crime, but I also believe it should fit the perpetrator. In fact, my colleague, Dr. Mark Cunningham of Seattle, was once asked on the witness stand to provide just *one* instance where he thought the death penalty would be justified. "Who, if anyone, Doctor, is the death penalty for?" asked the snarky prosecutor. Dr. Cunningham replied, "Someone like me. Someone who had good parents, attended good schools and was able to learn, got a good job and maybe had a family, and THEN went out and committed a deliberate, heinous crime. That's who the ultimate penalty should be reserved for." Bravo, Mark!

### "Richard"

Let me share a situation where issues like these became absolutely crucial to case resolution. I was asked to test a man charged with failure to register as a sex offender as mandated under the law. Failing to do so was both a new crime and a parole violation during the period of his parole supervision. As the result of my work in the "A" and "C" cases (see Chapter Nineteen), I had quite a bit of knowledge about the obligation to register, the wording of the instructions provided inmates, the standard procedure used to present this condition of parole to exiting prison inmates, their several-year obligation to report registration to their parole officers, and the need to register yearly for the rest of their lives once released from parole. So, here was "Richard," who registered while on parole, but stopped doing so when parole ended. I needed to explain this all too common scenario to the judge who would now decide the man's fate.

My assessment found that Richard had an IQ of 40 and was almost completely illiterate. As was the standard prison exit procedure at the time, he was called into his Correctional Counselor's office just prior to release and given brief verbal instructions. He was also handed a folder of release paperwork with Readability codings at and above the twelfth grade level. In other words, a person would need twelfth-grade reading ability to comprehend the content of the release packet. By the way, I know this is true because I was hired by the Board of Parole Hearings to code the Readability of almost seventy of the parole documents used in California and declared them unreadable for the vast majority of parolees. The Board then hired me to reword the forms to fifth and sixth grade levels which was a valiant effort; but even these edited forms still coded above the reading capability of people like Richard, who make up approximately one-third of prisoners and parolees.

Indeed, as a nonreader with a severely reduced IQ, Richard had totally blanked out during the verbal instructions by his prison release counselor. In our interview, he didn't even recall the occasion. Neither could he read the documents handed to him, but merely signed them as directed. As long as he was on parole, his agent reminded him to register yearly, "on your birthday," or close to it. But once parole ended, Richard made the same assumption I've seen many times over: he thought his obligation had also ended so, without support, simply faded into the woodwork. Before I came on this case, Richard was interviewed by three panel psychologists who produced one to two page reports of findings. One of them brought the wrong test which didn't measure at low enough levels to accurately portray Richard's very reduced IQ; the second used a definition of "mental deficiency" from the 1950s; and the third actually declared Richard "competent to stand trial." These so-called reports were not worth the paper they were printed on nor the money spent to obtain them. He now needed a full and accurate assessment of his capabilities.

My testimony in Richard's case involved explaining his skills profile to the Court, along with information about the counseling procedure at prison exit, and the Readability coding of the documents themselves. His Honor then deliberated a very short time before ruling in favor of the defense. Richard walked out of the courtroom a free man who had learned a valuable lesson that would prompt yearly registration for the rest of his life. In addition, we saved the taxpayer a small fortune that would have been wasted on re-incarcerating a man who simply needed reeducation.

I thought about Richard one day when I went to the local "Twin Towers" jail to test a detainee, only to find that a professional-looking man with a briefcase had beaten me to the front of the line. Since there was only one interior testing room, this could have punched a big hole in my schedule for the day, so I went over to see what was up.

I introduced myself, as did he and, yes, he was there to use the only interview room. I asked how long he might need it, thinking I could start my interview at the visitor's booth and then move downstairs when the other doctor vacated the room.

He mulled this over and said, "Well, let's see, I have two of them so ... *maybe an hour*."

"Oh," I said, "you're doing those little trial competency evaluations!"

(NOTE: These are the brief, flat pay interviews about trial-related concepts like those given to Richard, and just as valueless in my opinion.)

The man bristled and spat back, "Doctor, are you demeaning my work?"

(*Oops.*) "Of course not, I'm sorry," I said as I obsequiously slunk away. But I kicked myself later because here's what I *should* have said: *"Of course I'm demeaning a thirty-minute interview that will determine a man's fate. Shame on you for doing them in the first place!"*

**Slam Dunk**

Before I retire to the locker room, let me address some unfinished business that nags at me whenever I let it; namely, finding professionally-qualified replacements to duplicate my role in the justice system. In this pursuit, I once took on an intern at the request of a local psychologist who insisted that "Rachel's" education and career goals were similar to my own. As a result, I spent hours with the young woman sharing tests, reports, and general information which could equip her to step into the role. I then accepted five juvenile assessments in a neighboring county with plans to give Rachel some hands-on experience testing and/or report writing. That was precisely when she trotted off to Europe on a surprise vacation and later emailed me that they were extending the trip an extra week or two. Okay, I thought, these cases can wait a little longer. But then she sent me a second email with her great news: she was now getting married and leaving the profession! I didn't go to the wedding.

So, here is my parting shot: The justice system desperately needs experienced professionals who can conduct similar "psycho-educational" evaluations for use in guilt and penalty phase trials. At minimum, these people will need Ph.D. level training in special education or educational psychology, with cognate study in things like educational law, statistics, mental measurement, child development, and/or developmental psychology. They also need to have hands-on experience with the practical side of these issues through teaching or counseling individuals with a variety of special needs. In other words, ivory tower academicians need not apply because they lack real world knowledge of how individuals with disabilities function in everyday life.

This isn't just idle talk on my part, but a very real plea. I have been there and done that for almost thirty years. In this capacity, I have worked with dozens of highly competent and caring lawyers, some of whom earned the equivalent of a Master's degree in special education by the time their cases ended. In this way, we have changed the lives of hundreds of disabled defendants, inmates, and parolees for the better.

✧ ✧ ✧

Now, put down that latte and take up the fight.

## ABOUT THE AUTHOR

**Nancy Cowardin** received her Ph.D. degree in Educational Psychology from University of California at Los Angeles and served for nine years as Assistant Professor of Educational Psychology and Special Education at Whittier College and California State Polytechnic University.

Dr. Cowardin has directed grant programs sponsored by the California State Council on Developmental Disabilities, the Office of Criminal Justice Planning, the Los Angeles County Crime Subvention Program, and the Los Angeles Unified School District. Related projects insured accommodation services to a broad range of disabled individuals, from children enrolled in Head Start programs to youths and adults incarcerated for serious crimes. She has provided assessment and expert witness testimony in over 800 criminal cases, and served as the plaintiffs' principle expert in several class action lawsuits which secured, and now monitor, disability accommodations for inmates and parolees in the California prison system. She has been honored as "Educator of the Year" by the California Learning Disability Association for training more than 3,500 justice system professionals in identifying and accommodating disabilities in victims, witnesses and criminal defendants.

Now in retirement, Nancy operates Bodhi Gate Arts out of her home studio. She is a member of Hsi Lai Temple in Hacienda Heights, California, where she serves as a docent for tour groups and teaches classes in Buddhist arts. She regularly attends a Whittier-based writers' group and contributes memoirs to their bi-yearly publication.

# APPENDICES

# GLOSSARY OF TERMS

## A

**AAMR (AAIDD)** – American Association on Mental Retardation, now the AAIDD, American Association on Intellectual and Developmental Disabilities promotes progressive policies, sound research, effective practices and universal human rights for people with intellectual and developmental disabilities.

**ADA** – The Americans with Disabilities Act of 1990 is civil rights law that prohibits discrimination against individuals with disabilities in all areas of public life, including jobs, schools, transportation, and all public and private places that are open to the general public.

**Adaptive Behavior** – Defined by the AAIDD as the collection of conceptual, social, and practical skills that have been learned by people in order to function in their everyday lives.

**ADD/ADHD** – Both Attention Deficit Disorder and Attention Deficit Hyperactivity Disorder disrupt the sustained attention needed to intake new information for processing and integration with learned material. The D (deficit) factor implies spacey omissions; while the H (hyperactivity) factor usually leads to commissions based on impulsivity. (See Chapter Three for more information.)

**Ad-Seg** – Administrative Segregation units within prisons for inmates with disciplinary issues.

**Anomia** – Word-finding difficulties usually associated with left hemisphere brain trauma.

***Atkins v. Virginia*, *536 U.S. 304*** – *In 2002, the* U.S. Supreme Court ruled 6-3 that executing people with intellectual disabilities violates the Eighth Amendment's ban on cruel and unusual punishments, but allowed states the discretion to define who has intellectual disability. Twelve years later in *Hall v. Florida,* the Court narrowed the discretion under which U.S. states can designate an individual convicted of murder as too intellectually incapacitated to be executed.

## C

**Class Action Lawsuit** – Any lawsuit where the verdict will pertain to an entire "class" of similar individuals rather than a single plaintiff.

**Cognitive Disabilities** – Disabilities that affect and limit learning, thinking, and understanding under federal and state laws. In schools, these disabilities are Specific Learning Disability, Intellectual Disability, and depending on severity, Attention Deficit Disorder.

**Commissions** – Refers to false positive responses associated with impulsivity. (See Chapter Three for more information.)

**Compensatory Skills** – A variety of alternative and/or self-help behaviors employed by people with disabilities to mask their deficits in social settings. One example might be wearing a broken watch in order to have the excuse to ask someone else for the time.

**Composite IQ Score** – The combined score for both verbal and performance portions of an IQ test.

**Cultural-Familial Retardation** – Intellectual disabilities that cannot be explained by genetics, birth trauma, or subsequent brain insult, but instead result from a family's cultural, religious, or social practices. (See Chapter Eight for more information.)

# D

**DD 1, 2, and 3** – California prisons determine the support needs of incoming inmates during the reception process, labeling those with intellectual disabilities as DD1 (mild level), DD2 (moderate needs), or DD3 extensive support needs). DD2 and DD3 inmates are generally housed in one of eight designated prisons with specially-trained staff.

**Developmental Disability/Developmental Delay** – The developmental disabilities served by the California Regional Center system include: Intellectual Disability, Cerebral Palsy, Autism, and Epilepsy. A developmental disability must occur prior to age 18 (in the developmental period) and affect at least 25% of the individual's function. Other sources tend to use the term synonymous with Intellectual Disability or, in the past, mental retardation.

**Differential Standard Diploma** – A nonstandard diploma awarded special education students based on the individualized plans designed by a school-based (IEP) team. Where applied, qualifying disabled students are exempted from taking typical competency tests as long as they met IEP goals.

**Distractibility** – The inability to sustain attention to a target due to fragmented attention to peripheral conditions. Distractibility is a hallmark of ADD and ADHD.

**Diversion** – Monitored *diversion services* are sometimes extended in lieu of prison, especially if the defendant is disabled. Diversion usually involves a secure group home setting and classes to improve behavior. It is monitored by a county's Probation Department, with frequent updates to the referring court.

**Due Process** – The legal requirement that the state must respect all legal rights that are owed to a person. When a governmental agency causes harms to a person without following the exact course of the law, this constitutes a due process violation under the Fifth and Fourteenth Constitutional Amendments.

**Dyslexia** – An inborn inability to automatically process the written symbol system needed for reading and/or writing.

## E

**Educable Mentally Retarded** – Old term for classes made up of children with IQs of about 55 to 70 who are thought to require "mild" supports to function at maximum capacity. The curriculum included basic academic education along with some domestic, leisure, and vocational skills.

**Executive Decision-making/Executive Brain** – Refers to brain functions that are organizational and managerial, usually associated with the frontal lobes. A healthy "executive" takes charge of decision-making and monitors the outcome, rather than relying on impulse or luck.

**Expressive Language** – The ability to locate and express word labels, string words into sentences, and provide oral explanations, content, or answers on cue.

## F

**Flat Skills Profile** – Refers to the flat arrangement of scores usually seen in students/clients with intellectual disabilities. This score spread contains few or no skill "spikes" of improved ability, but instead shows below average skills across the board.

**Forensic Assessor** – The term "forensic" refers to the application of any specialty or discipline as it may relate to the law. As such, there are forensic accountants and forensic dentists, etc., as well as the more traditional forensic pathologists or forensic psychologists. My title as a forensic assessor pertains to the provision of psychoeducational evaluations for use at trials and sentencing hearings.

**Fundamental Fairness** – A rule that applies the principles of due process to a judicial proceeding. It insures fair and equal treatment to all persons regardless of individual differences or disability.

## G

**GED Diploma** – A high school diploma earned through self-study and written examination.

**GED Tutors** – In prisons, GED tutors assist peer inmates in earning GED diplomas. As such, they earn special status and are usually "paid" with canteen items, protection, or other favors.

***Gladys R.* Questionnaire** – The California Supreme Court ruled *In Re Gladys R.* that minors under age 14 require additional questioning at arrest to insure their understanding. The four question interview is intended to determine whether the child (or mentally young suspect) understands right versus wrong and the consequences of admitting guilt.

**Group Home** – Adult consumers with Intellectual Disabilities (and other Regional Center clients) are often placed in small group homes as a move toward independent living. These are Regional Center vendored and staffed by qualified caregivers.

**Guilt Phase of Trial** – Trial portion that determines whether the defendant has committed a purposeful crime. In capital (death penalty) cases, this first phase is followed by a “penalty phase” to determine punishment.

## H

***Habeas (Corpus)*** – Latin meaning literally “produce the body” is a recourse in law whereby a person can report an unlawful detention or imprisonment and request a court hearing to determine whether the detention should continue. *Habeas* cases usually refer to death penalty (or other sentence) appeals.

**Hyper Alertness/Hyper Vigilance** – See Vigilance, below.

## I

**IEP, IEP Team** – The Individualized Educational Plan (or Individualized Learning Plan - ILP) is created by a school-based or other team of professionals and is a binding contract between the parent/child and provider for services toward identified goals.

**Impulsivity** – Characterized as fast, bad decisions and associated with ADHD. (See Chapter Three for more information.)

**Incapable** – In some states, young and mentally young defendants may be considered “incapable” of committing a knowing and purposeful crime due to their cognitive limitations.

**Incompetence (Incompetent to Stand Trial)** – Incompetence is based on mental limitations that preclude the ability to assist one’s lawyer, self-advocate in one’s own defense, and behave properly in court. Mental illness, intellectual disability, and certain other incapacitating conditions may call trial competence into question.

**Information Processing** – The chain of cognitive processes that facilitates the intake, association, storage, retrieval, and expression of information through the senses.

**Intellectual Disability (ID)** – A disability characterized by significant limitations in *both* intellectual functioning and adaptive behavior. This disability typically originates before the age of 18 and undermines many everyday conceptual, social and practical skills.

**Internal Language** – Language also termed "private speech" that one conducts internally as a means of self-guidance.

## K

**Karyotype** – Karyotype depicts the chromosome count of an organism and what these chromosomes look like under a light microscope. Attention is paid to their length, banding pattern, any differences between the sex chromosomes, and any other physical characteristics.

## L

**Language Processing** – Refers to a breakdown in the chain of mental abilities needed to smoothly process oral (or sometimes written) language. Errors can occur at Intake, during Medial phase association, and/or at Output where self-expression is thwarted.

**Learning Disability/Specific Learning Disability** – Generally refers to a "significant" discrepancy between one's actual performance and expectation (based on his or her intelligence) in one or more of the basic academic and/or processing skills. A Specific LD usually means only one or two skills are depressed; while a Pervasive LD suggests all functions are discrepant. (See Chapter One for more information.)

**Limited Alertness** – This is just another way to describe "distractibility" or, lapses in attention, while attending to a task. Limited alertness is associated with the Omissions factor in the attentional deviations we call ADD or ADHD. (See Chapter Three for more information.)

**Literacy Standard** – The national literacy standard for reading and comprehending simple adult materials is about the 5th grade level. Most local newspapers and pop magazines can be read and understood by youths and adults functioning at this level. But, to comprehend higher level documents, government forms, contracts, textbooks, and the like, a far higher literacy standard is indicated. Prison inmates in California fall fairly evenly into three groups: Functionally illiterate (Pre-Primer to 4th grade level reading), Basic Literacy (5th to 7th grade levels), and full literacy (high school reading levels). However, even this highest level is not sufficient to smoothly comprehend the more complex forms and materials mentioned above.

**LWOPP** – The Life WithOut the Possibility of Parole sentence awarded by a court or jury, usually in a penalty phase trial.

## M

**Mental Age (MA)** – These particular test scores are designed to make comparisons with a specified range of chronological ages. Mental Age (MA) scores allow us to make accurate statements comparing the thinking, learning, and understanding of a given test subject with those of his chronological agemates. This is how assessors determine that someone's thinking capability is on a par with younger (or older) test subjects.

**Mental Retardation** – Antiquated term now updated to ID (see above) that requires significantly subaverage performance in *both* intellectual and adaptive skills. The disability group was divided into levels characterized as "mild" (IQs of 55-70), "moderate" (IQs of 40-55), "Severe" (IQs of 25-40), and "Profound" (IQs below 25, or untestable).

**Miranda Admonition** – The statement of Constitutional Rights that must be read to criminal defendants before formal police interrogation can begin. One commonly used form of the admonition states: *You have the right to remain silent; anything you say can and will be used against you in a court of law; you have the right to an attorney; if you cannot afford one, an attorney will be provided free of charge. Understanding these rights, do you wish to talk with me (us)?*

## N

**Nonverbal IQ** – Intelligence measured by nonlingual test content such as picture and pattern matching, logical sequencing, and item recognition.

**Normalization** – A nationwide movement to return individuals with disabilities into the mainstream of society. Efforts here include finding and monitoring independent living arrangements, on-the-job shadowing, and advanced educational opportunities through "adult" training programs.

## O

**Omissions** – Refers to cyclic and/or accumulated lapses of attention associated with a true Attention *Deficit* Disorder. (See Chapter Three for additional information.)

**Overlearning** – This term refers to the practice of teaching, re-teaching, and checking for understanding that is used in many or most special education classrooms to improve what we call "durability of learning." Without it, many of our students will soon forget and/or discard previously learned material. The phrase, "five steps ahead, four steps back" refers to the weekly erosion of newly-learned material unless this practice is upheld.

## P

**Parole Conditions** – Usually refers to meeting pre-set standards in everyday programming (educational and vocational skills) and discipline while serving the specified prison term. A final parole condition requires adequate plans for community and vocational reintegration once the inmate leaves prison.

**Parole Revocation** – Formal process by which one's parole is revoked due to an infraction. Revocations require due process of law and a formal hearing, with counsel if desired, to review and/or plead to charges.

**Penalty Phase of Trial** – Secondary trial phase to determine whether a defendant found guilty of a capital crime is now eligible for the death penalty.

**Performance IQ** – Intelligence measured by non-lingual means such as pattern-matching, the application of logic, and making visual discriminations. See also Nonverbal IQ.

**Pragmatic Language** – Refers to everyday, functional language with practical and social intent.

**Preoperational Children** – Developmental stage of children, approximately four to seven years of age, who have not yet established concrete operational thought.

**Presupposition** – The ability to make logical assumptions based on all available information and to act accordingly. (See Chapter Five for a more in-depth discussion.)

**Private Speech** – Internal language-based thought processes used to guide actions and decision-making.

**Psychoeducational Assessment** – Refers to a battery of tests that cover thinking ability, accumulated academic learning, and the language and information processing skills that facilitate learning in a given test subject.

## R

**Readability** – Refers to how readable and at what level a document can be comprehended. Readability formulas consider not only length of sentences, but the number of "common" and multi-syllable words in written text. Analyses of these sorts then determine the grade and age levels needed for full comprehension.

**Reception Centers** – Intake centers where new inmates are assessed for permanent prison placement.

**Receptive Language** – The ability to perceive, understand, and process written and/or oral language (directed toward you) on cue.

## S

**Sentencing Advocate** – Forensic specialists who assist attorneys with procedures such as jury selection, case and/or client preparation for testimony, hiring experts, etc.

**SHU** – Refers to the Secure Handling Unit inside jails and prisons that is usually reserved for prisoners with problematic behavior. SHU locations may be utilized for temporary (disciplinary infractions) or permanent (certain gang members) housing.

**Specific Learning Disability** – A disability characterized by average intellectual functioning, but "significant" discrepancies (see below) in one or more academic, language, or processing subskills.

**Significant Discrepancy** – Any skill demonstrating a 22 point lag from expectancy based on the earned IQ number.

**Special Day Class** – Team-determined placement in a segregated special class for more than 50% of the school day. SCD students may be "mainstreamed" out for elective subjects, but usually remain in the specialized setting for academic learning. If less than 50% of a student's day requires this specialized setting for instruction, he or she is usually placed in the Resource Specialist (pull-out) Program.

**Spiky Profile** – Charted skills profile showing extreme highs and lows across test batteries. Spiky score arrangements are typically seen in students with Specific Learning Disabilities.

**Standard Deviation (SD)** – SDs measure how close a score falls to the population "average" of 100. The *variance* for a particular test can be as few as 2 or 3 points, or range as high as 10 or 15 points depending on its norming data. Smaller variations allow for greater confidence in making statements about a subject's performance relative to everyone else in his or her age band.

**Standard Scores** - Standard Scores earned on tests allow us to place the test taker into wide bands within the normal population. Using this distribution, 68% of scores will fall in high- and low-average bands, while 26% will be equally divided between below- and above-average bands. The remaining 6% of scores fall in either severely subaverage (3%) or well above-average ("gifted" = 3%) bands.

# T

**Test Protocols** – Refers to the actual test documents administered to a referred subject. Protocols are usually printed by a test company after adequate norming procedures, and are accompanied by charts of data allowing comparisons to others in the age band.

**Trainable Mentally Retarded** – Old term for classes made up of children with IQs of about 40 to 55 who are thought to require "moderate" supports to function at maximum capacity. The curriculum included only minimal academic education, with greater focus on domestic, leisure, and vocational skills.

**Traumatic Brain Injury (TBI)** – Physical insult to the brain through accident or toxins that results in disabilities that resemble formal Intellectual Disabilities. TBI is a Category V condition for admission to the California Regional Center system, but only if it occurred prior to age 18.

**Trial Competence** – The ability to participate knowingly and intelligently as a self-advocate during the trial process. Trial competence requires understanding of the case facts, how to assist defense counsel, the Constitutional Rights waived at arrest and now as a defendant in Court, proper Courtroom behavior, and possible penalties that may result from participation.

**Trustees** – Jail or prison inmates chosen by correctional staff as helpers typically due to both their lesser charges at intake and exemplary behavior while incarcerated.

# V

**Verbal IQ** – Intelligence based on language usage, language-based logic, and associated problem-solving.

**Vigilance** – The process of remaining alert during specific tests of attention so as to eliminate both Omissions of stimuli and Commissions of false positives. So-called Hyper-vigilance can assist a test taker for the short term, but is difficult to apply over time.

**Visual Learner** – A learner who depends on and utilizes his or her stronger visual (seeing and doing), rather than weaker language-based (listening and speaking) processing skills in tackling academic material.

# APPENDIX A
# Special Education ABCs

Cumulative record and medical files of identified special education students may include terms and acronyms such as the following. Outdated terms that I sometimes found in older case files are included in this listing.

Basic Categories of Exceptionality:

| | |
|---|---|
| * CH | Communicative Handicap |
| * LH | Learning Handicap |
| * PH | Physical Handicap |
| * SH | Severe Handicap |

Specific Diagnoses:

| | |
|---|---|
| * ADD | Attention Deficit Disorder |
| * ADHD | Attention Deficit (with) Hyperactivity Disorder |
| * BD | Behavior Disordered (SBD - Severe Behavior Disorder) |
| * DD | Developmental Disability |
| * EH | Educationally Handicapped |
| * EMR | Educable Mentally Retarded (*outdated term*) |
| * HOH | Hard of Hearing |
| * ID | Intellectually Disabled |
| * LD | Learning Disability (also LDG — Learning Disability Group) |
| * OH | Orthopedic Handicap |
| * OHI | Other Health Impairment |
| * SED | Severe Emotional Disturbance (or ED - Emotionally Disturbed) |
| * S/L | Speech/Language Disorder |
| * TMR | Trainable Mentally Retarded (*outdated term*) |
| * VH | Visual Handicap |

General Diagnoses:

- * IWEN — Individual With Exceptional Needs (All disabilities)

School-Based Service Contract:

- * IEP — Individualized Educational Plan/Program
- * ILP — Individualized Learning Plan
- * IPP — Individualized Program Plan

Services Provided:

- * APE — Adaptive Physical Education
- * DIS — Designated Instructional Services
- * LAS — Language and/or Speech Services
- * OT — Occupational Training/Therapy
- * PT — Physical Therapy
- * VR — Vocational Rehabilitation

Where Services are provided:

- * HH — Home/Hospital Services
- * RCP — Regular Class Program
- * RSP — Resource Specialist Program (<50% of the school day)
- * SDC — Special Day Class (50% or more of the school day)

## The ABC's of Government and Advocacy

- AAMR — American Association on Mental Retardation (*outdated term*, now AAIDD-AA on Intellectual & Developmental Disabilities)
- ACLD — Association for Children and Adults with Learning Disabilities
- ADA — Americans with Disabilities Act of 1990
- APA — American Psychiatric Association
- ASHA — American Speech-Language-Hearing Association
- AT/ATD — Assistive Technology/Assistive Technology Device

| | |
|---|---|
| CAP | Continuum of Alterative Placements |
| CASE | Council of Administrators of Special Education |
| CBM | Curriculum-Based Measurements *-OR-* Cognitive Behavior Modification |
| CEC | Council for Exceptional Children |
| CFR | Code of Federal Regulations |
| CLD | Council for Learning Disabilities |
| CNS | Central Nervous System |
| CP | Cerebral Palsy |
| DE | (U.S.) Department of Education |
| DLD/CEC | Division for Learning Disabilities/Council for Exceptional Children |
| DSM | Diagnostic and Statistical Manual of Mental Disorders (*American Psychiatric Association publication and guide*) |
| FAPE | Free Appropriate Public Education (per federal mandate) |
| GATE | Gifted and Talented Education |
| IDEA | Individuals with Disabilities Education Act |
| IEP | Individualized Educational Plan/Program |
| IEPT | Individualized Educational Plan Team |
| IFSP | Individualized Family Service Plan |
| IPP | Individualized Program Plan |
| LDA | Learning Disability Association (formerly the ACLD) |
| LEA | Local Education Agency (school district or local planning unit) |
| LEP | Limited English Proficient |

| | |
|---|---|
| LRA | Least Restrictive Alternative (for behavior management) |
| LRE | Least Restrictive Environment (for placement) |
| MBD | Minimal Brain Dysfunction |
| MGM | Mentally Gifted Minor (now, Gifted and Talented) |
| NAPAS | National Association of Protection and Advocacy Systems |
| NASP | National Association of School Psychologists |
| NCLD | National Center for Learning Disabilities |
| NICHD | National Center of Child Health and Human Development |
| NIH | National Institute of Health |
| OCR | Office of Civil Rights |
| OSEP | Office of Special Education Programs |
| OSERS | Office of Special Education and Rehabilitative Services |
| P&A | Protection & Advocacy |
| PDD | Pervasive Developmental Disorder |
| PLD | Pervasive Learning Disability |
| RLA | Responsible Local Agency (a county or local school district) |
| SEA | State Education Agency |
| SIT | Sensory Integration Therapy |
| TBI | Traumatic Brain Injury |

* Source: Learning Disability Association of California

# APPENDIX B
## Arrest Interview Transcripts

The following exchanges are taken from arrest interviews involving mentally or chronologically young, intellectually or learning disabled, and/or language delayed defendants. Some were as young as seven years of age, yet police officers forged ahead with a line of questioning that baffles many adults placed in the same position. As you read these exchanges, ask yourself if the defendant a) truly understands the abstract content regarding one's "rights" and the ability to "waive" them; b) has enough knowledge to freely waive counsel and/or his or her rights; and c) has any clue as to the effects his cooperation here will have on the immediate case and his future.

### Interview #1: Jay, Age 7, ADD

Let's start with a review of the interrogation of Jay (Chapter Eighteen) where, solely due to his young age, the officers are delivering the so-called "Gladys R" interview as a follow-up to his *Yes*, *Yes*, and *Yes* answers to the standard Miranda Admonition. Jay was accused of arson.

Officer: Do you know the difference between right and wrong?
Jay: Un huh.
Officer: Name something that's right to do.
Jay: Go to school.
Officer: Name something that's wrong to do.
Jay: Fire.
Officer: What happens if you light a fire?
Jay: You get in trouble.

Does Jay understand that "fire," in and of itself, is not actually "wrong"? Sometimes, lighting a fire is a safe and necessary thing to do, but Jay's limited experience tells him otherwise. The final question is very telling in terms of this child's understanding about the actual dangers of a fire out of control. Here, he sees the "problem" only from his own perspective—he's in trouble. This is developmentally equivalent to a same-age child who insists: "The clouds follow me when I walk"—It's all about him.

**Interview #2: Allen, Age 13, LD**

In Allen's case, the officers begin with the *Miranda* warning and are so content with the results, that they choose not to administer the *Gladys R* interview as a follow-up.

Officer: Do you know about rights? Have you ever heard about them? From TV or anywhere else?
Allen: Kind of.
Officer: Okay. You have the right not to talk to me. Do you understand?
Allen: I can talk to you?
Officer: You have the right ... it's a right. And then anything you say can be used against you in court. These are your rights. And you have the right to talk to an attorney.
Allen: Is that a lawyer?
Officer: Right! You have that right, too. So those are your rights. And after I've told you your rights, do you want to talk to me?
Allen: I don't know.
Officer: You don't know?
Allen: Yeah.
Officer: You do want to, or you don't?
Allen: Yeah.
Officer: Yes? You want to talk to me some more?
Okay, sign your name right here (on the Miranda waiver).

Allen then signed the waiver, and with it, signed his life away with no parent or attorney present. It makes me wonder what pictures were running through his mind regarding being *right*, waving his *right* (hand), and having a third kind of *right* like the policeman says people have on TV. This is confusing for someone only beginning to develop an understanding of abstract terms and concepts.

### Interview #3: Charles, Age 19, ID

This intellectually-disabled, and therefore mentally-young, defendant was a chronological adult at the time of his arrest and was therefore administered the standard Miranda warning. He has enough street knowledge to know that he should ask for an attorney, but is easily discouraged from exercising this right by the interviewing officer.

| | |
|---|---|
| Charles: | So, uh, do I need an attorney in this case? |
| Officer: | Well, no. What I'm saying is that we want you to talk about this, OK? |
| Charles: | OK. Pardon me, sir, but I don't want to be a guilty [person]. I don't have no attorney or no one to back me up or nothing. I don't know how this stuff goes. |
| Officer: | All right. Do you wish to give up your right to remain silent? In other words, do you want to talk to us and give your side of the story? |
| Charles: | I'm just trying to say with the attorney part, I'm trying to say, uh, do I need my attorney right here with me? |
| Officer: | Well, I can't tell you what you should and shouldn't do. |
| Charles: | I mean, I really want to talk to my attorney too, though. |
| Officer: | So, you want an attorney here before you talk to us? Is that what you're telling me? |
| Charles: | Well, can he come here right now? |

Officer: No. I mean, we can't get an attorney for you right now. You'll have an attorney later on when you go to court.
Charles: OK. Well, then, I'll talk to you all. I'll talk to you.

Does Charles ask for a lawyer? Let me count the ways ... Yet, this conversation resulted in a signed waiver and the State of California filing a capital case against the intellectually-disabled defendant. Whenever I speak about *"fundamental fairness"* for people with disabilities, this interview comes to mind as one egregious example of the alternative.

**Interview #4: Damon, Age 13, LD/LAS**

This youth was being interrogated without a parent or lawyer present despite rather obvious signs that learning and/or language disabilities were present. Take a look at the following exchange:

Officer: Were her legs clothed (sees the blank look on Damon's face) or were they ... were they bare?
Damon: They were, ah, they closed.
Officer: They were clothed?
Damon: They were closed.
Officer: Closed?
Damon: Yes.

It takes several tries using related terms for these unequal conversational partners to finally find common ground:

Officer: Did she have clothes on or ... was she naked?
Damon: She had clothes on.

At some point, the officer sees the reduced language capability of the youth and begins to supply needed words to facilitate the flow of the conversation:

Officer: Okay. What did you pick up when you went inside the house?
Damon: It was like a little ... little hook thingy.
Officer: A knife ... did it have a blade on it?
Damon: No, it was a little hook.
Officer: Okay. Do you know what a sickle is?
Damon. No.

Indeed, it is tempting to provide words for one so limited in scope; however, the continuation of this exchange demonstrates the insertion of something far more incriminating than single words in this dangerously leading conversation:

Officer: And, um, so the reason you picked that up is in case you encountered somebody in the house?
Damon: Yes.*

* Damon's agreement with this final statement is explainable when you realize that he had no idea of what the word "encountered" means. I know this because I included it in his vocabulary test during our subsequent assessment session. His response here demonstrates the need for external guidance and approval seen in most defendants with language and cognitive disabilities. Had the officer substituted words like "came across somebody" instead of "encountered" Damon might have told a very different story.

# APPENDIX C
## Sample Declaration

GS (CA Bar #)
Pasadena, California
Attorney for Defendant: LJG

UNITED STATES DISTRICT COURT

CENTRAL DISTRICT OF CALIFORNIA

WESTERN DIVISION

| | | |
|---|---|---|
| UNITED STATES OF AMERICA, | ) | NO. CR 07-XXX(C)-DDP |
| | ) | |
| Plaintiff, | ) | DECLARATION OF NANCY |
| | ) | COWARDIN, Ph.D.; EXHIBIT A |
| v | ) | |
| LJG, | ) | |
| | ) | |
| Defendant. | ) | |
| | ) | |
| | ) | |
| ______________________________ | ) | |

I, Nancy Cowardin, Ph.D., state and declare the following:

1. I am an educational diagnostician and former teacher credentialed by the State of California with specific expertise in cognitive and learning disorders. Exhibit A attached hereto is a true and correct copy of my curriculum vitae which lists my education, experience and qualifications.

2. On October 21, 2010, I conducted a psycho-educational assessment of LJG in a private interview room at the Metropolitan Detention Center in Los Angeles, California. My assessment included approximately four hours of direct testing and observation of Ms. G to assess her current functioning in terms of intelligence, academic achievement, expressive and receptive language, information processing, and several applied skills that promote adult independence. I also reviewed the charges against Ms. G and miscellaneous medical records covering 2008 to 2010. In the absence of formal school records, additional interviews with Dr. V C, staff from the Lanterman Regional Center, and the client herself supplied basic information regarding her prior educational placements and diagnostic classification.

3. I concluded that Ms. G has several conceptual deficits that are consistent with the developmental disability known as mental retardation as defined by the American Association on Intellectual and Developmental Disabilities. I administered the Kaufman Brief Intelligence Test (KBIT2) to Ms. G which quantified a composite intelligence quotient (IQ) of 66 and places her in the bottom one percent of persons in her peer group. Although her full scale and verbal IQ scores of 66 and 68 fall within the range for clear qualification, her performance score of 74 falls in a slightly better "borderline" range. This latter score nevertheless codes below some 96% of a population of same-aged test subjects.

4. My finding that Ms. G suffers from mental retardation with "mild" support needs is corroborated by an independent psychological evaluation of Ms. G conducted by TC, Ph.D. on October 15, 2008, approximately eight months prior to her arrest on the federal racketeering charges. My post-assessment review of this report indicates that Dr. TC administered the Leiter International Performance Scale-Revised and concluded that Ms. G has "mild mental retardation" based on a Full-Scale IQ Composite Score of 57.

5. Ms. G reads individual words and comprehends prose material at a third-grade level. These primer level skills tabulate the mental age equivalent of a child who is eight and one-half years old. As such, her ability to comprehend text falls in the bottom one percent of persons in her age group. This conclusion is based on my administration of the (word) Recognition and (text) Comprehension subtests of the Kaufman Test of Educational Achievement (KTEA-II).

6. My finding that Ms. G reads at a third-grade level is also corroborated by Dr. TC's independent psychological evaluation. Here, his administration of the Wide Range Achievement Test - Revision III determined a similar third-grade level score.

7. Ms. G also has a significant language processing deficit which is consistent with school-based classification as one with a severe Learning Handicap. Her expressive and receptive vocabulary is equivalent to that of a six-to-seven-year old and is characterized by difficulty producing answers on demand *and* confusion receiving communicative intent from even simple utterances offered by others. Her auditory processing is severely impaired, and her ability to process verbal information is equivalent to that of a four-and-one-half-year-old child.

8. I have reviewed the "Consent to Search" form dated June 16, 2009, which Ms. G purportedly signed. This form has a mid-sixth grade readability index and a language age of eleven and one-half years. Because Ms. G reads at a third-grade level, it is unlikely that she would have fully comprehended the nature of the rights she was waiving or the consequences of waiving these rights even if she had attempted to read the form. Additionally, even if the "Consent to Search" form had been read to her, Ms. G's vocabulary and auditory processing deficits would tend to negate full comprehension of the rights she was waiving and the consequences of waiving them.

9. I have reviewed the "Advice of Rights" form dated June 16, 2009, which Ms. G purportedly signed. The *Miranda* rights version printed on this form has a readability coding at grade 7.7 and language age just above age twelve and one-half years. Even if the form had been read to Ms. G, her six-to-seven year age score for single word vocabulary and four-and-one-half-year age score for auditory processing would tend to negate full comprehension of her *Miranda* rights and the consequences of waiving them. The multiple utterances that constitute this *Miranda* rights version (9 consecutive sentences without typical checks for understanding) present additional difficulties for one functioning at a reduced language level. I have found that, under such circumstances, impaired individuals tend to feign comprehension rather than disclose their deficits to others. In this particular case, it is unlikely that Ms. G would interpret more than the gist of an oral *Miranda* advisement due to her ongoing processing imprecision. Moreover, because Ms. G reads at a third-grade level, she could not fully comprehend the *Miranda* advisement even if she had attempted to read the form.

I declare under penalty of perjury under the laws of the United States of America that the foregoing is true and correct. Executed on this 20th day of June 2011.

NANCY COWARDIN, Ph.D.

# APPENDIX D
# Descriptive Table of Contents

## Preface

This section introduces my work as a forensic assessor with particular expertise in the cognitive disabilities that impact thinking, learning, and understanding. This twenty-five year career in the nationwide criminal justice system began with "Omar," a dyslexic high school student who stabbed the English teacher who insisted he read in front of the class. Omar's successful case outcome opened the door to my first death penalty case (John, Chapter Five) only a few weeks later.

## Ground Rules

This section lays out six fundamental ground rules that I refined working with lawyers, courts, and correctional staff in more than seven hundred fifty cases. These rules cover things such as decoding the true intention of legal referrals, minimizing hassles at prison entry, the importance of being a "straight shooter," and acknowledging the humanity of both guards and inmates in jail and prison environments. Actual cases and experiences are used to illustrate the importance of these practical tips in building an ethical and successful career.

## PART ONE: Learning, Attention, and Language Disabilities

## Chapter One: J.R., Eight Years on Death Row

This foundational chapter defines Learning Disabilities as a syndrome and describes how the personal disorganization associated with related disorders can lead to criminal involvement. It features "J.R.," an eighteen-year-old youth with compound learning, attention, and language disabilities, whose bungled robbery attempt landed him on death row at Louisiana's Angola Prison. Our successful appeal eight years later resulted in his transfer to the general prison population. The significant improvements J.R. made through a diligent program of self-study captured the attention of the Warden, who arranged for his appointment as a peer tutor in the prison's GED classes.

## Chapter Two: James, A Story of Perseveration

Due to his huge size and brute strength, James sometimes assisted his brother with plumbing demolition jobs, this one, at the home of a single female teacher. A few days later, James returned to the home on his bicycle, let himself in using the key from his brother's plumbing truck, and began to fill large trash bags with the woman's belongings. Things escalated out of control when James' longstanding learning and attention deficits derailed his plan for a hasty exit and the owner returned home.

## Chapter Three: Carl, Disorganization and Impulsivity

The attention deficit disorder well known to Carl's family soon became apparent to his basketball coach and teammates, all of whom testified that he required assistance to carry out multi-step plays. This same pattern of disorganization was seen in the surveillance video that filmed his botched attempt at a convenience store robbery several years later. Here, the clerk's refusal to cooperate with Carl's commands triggered the knee-jerk reaction that resulted in capital murder charges.

## Chapter Four: Danny, ADHD and a Loaded Gun

Banished from his mother's home after an argument, fourteen-year-old Danny was forced to live with his biological father. He then found himself entering high school in a new town without the support of his longstanding ADHD medication. Sent home for a disciplinary infraction, he accessed a gun from a storage cabinet and hid it under his bedcovers. As Danny contemplated suicide, his antsy fingers discharged the gun several times that afternoon. The final shot accidentally killed his half-sister.

## Chapter Five: John, Bungled Copy-Cat Burglary

John attempted to copy the burglary scheme that had been successfully used by an acquaintance, but almost immediately veered off track with disastrous results. He was arrested at the bank the following Monday, trying to cash the check written to him by the now deceased victim. Under interrogation, his compound learning and language disorders led to several naive denials, multiple two-way miscommunications, and a confession easily coerced by police through threats of abandonment.

## Chapter Six: Gil, Bragging to Impress

Lumpy, overweight, and Learning Disabled Gil made the perfect patsy for the cute undercover detective investigating a gang murder in his neighborhood. Bragging to impress her, the twenty-five-year-old claimed a gang affiliation he did not have, plus first-hand knowledge of the murder. Subsequently, a gang leader cooperating with local police for a reduced sentence visited Gil to dangle threats of bodily harm if he did not assume the blame. The ruse worked like a charm, and he found himself on trial as the shooter.

## Chapter Seven: Lenny, Mock Jury Trial

Lenny had already served twenty years for the accidental shooting of a security guard when a state-level team took up his case on appeal. Current testing revealed compound learning, language, and auditory impairments that were not disclosed at his initial trial. The team therefore arranged two mock juries to re-hear the case with the addition of this information just prior to his actual re-trial. In light of the new and unequivocal disability evidence, both the mock and actual juries found him ineligible for the death penalty. Time served satisfied the sentencing requirement for his now reduced charge.

## PART TWO: Intellectual Disabilities

### Chapter Eight: Tina, Confused Sexual Boundaries

This foundational chapter discusses genetic versus cultural-familial causation in presenting the case of Tina and her inbred family, all of whom demonstrated mild to severe Intellectual Disabilities. The thirty-six-year-old was charged with failure to prevent the molestation of her two daughters by her husband, brothers, and a family friend. Advocacy with New York's criminal justice system was needed, first, to explain Tina's generalized incompetence as a defendant; and, second, to shed light on her understandable confusion regarding sexual boundaries as the victim of paternal incest.

### Chapter Nine: Ronny, A Story of Compassion

This Intellectually Disabled man was first attracted to a woman at a bus stop and later followed her home. At the suggestion of his gang involved brothers, he entered her home one night, and things spiraled out of control. He was found guilty of her murder, and the death penalty was considered. Upon hearing testimony about his pervasive disabilities, however, the jury opted for mercy, as did the mother of his victim.

### Chapter Ten: Dee, Much Needed Life Supports

Dee's chapter is actually the abbreviated psychoeducational report used by the defense to obtain a successful outcome in her federal trial on gang-related charges. Disability findings in this same report also secured Dee's admission to the California Regional Center system. This is one case where a brush with the justice system led to much-needed reeducation and life supports, vocational assistance, and an expanded social network of appropriate friendships.

### Chapter Eleven: Crimes of Innocence

Brief vignettes focus on twenty-year-old Anna, lured into sexual behavior by a local junior high school boy, and twenty-eight-year-old Jimmy, who had inappropriately touched several children in his mother's daycare program as an adolescent. A third vignette introduces Ed, who repeated the deviant sexual experiences he suffered as a patient growing up in a New York institution. The chapter points out that people with Intellectual Disabilities are far more likely to be the victims than the perpetrators of sexual abuse. In this regard, it is estimated that the average person with ID will experience thirteen sexual assaults over his or her lifetime.

## Chapter Twelve: Colin, Cruel and Unusual Punishment

Colin lived in constant fear as his fellow death row inmates periodically joined together to trick and terrify him by stating that "today is the day" of his execution. He would then tearfully wait for guards to come and take him away, only to conclude at bedtime that there had been a delay. A patiently crafted pro-bono appeal based on testing, file review, and family interviews resulted in his release to the general prison population after twenty years of such abuse.

## Chapter Thirteen: Earl, Toxic Exposure

Earl's *habeas* case was one of six filed in the state of Oklahoma following the Supreme Court's 2002 Atkins decision. His death row appeal was based on longstanding evidence of mental retardation due to years of exposure to toxic metals in the soil, air, and ground water of the Super Fund site surrounding his home town. A visit to the area clearly explained the ghost town that now stands in its place; however, the decision to evacuate came too late for victims like Earl, who continue to suffer the consequences.

## Chapter Fourteen: The Rape of Anita

A lapse in supervision by her one-to-one aide led to Anita's rape by an apparent transient loitering on her school campus.

Unfortunately, like many other victims with Intellectual Disabilities, she could provide little descriptive information, thus the crime went unsolved. Subsequent conversations about the attack demonstrated Anita's continuing confusion differentiating normal sexuality from exploitation and abuse. Her experience highlights the crucial need for better sex education programs for individuals functioning at reduced cognitive levels.

## PART THREE: Other Issues

### Chapter Fifteen: Ian, Severe Behavior Disorder

Although Ian's Severe Behavior Disorder was well known to most school staff, a substitute teacher's refusal to honor his IEP "cool-out" option threw the youth into crisis. A duplicate incident only weeks later led to a nose-to-nose confrontation with a vice principal who later filed criminal charges. Court advocacy for this youth resulted in a reduced penalty and his transfer to an alternative high school that would deal more appropriately with his behavioral differences. A discussion of public school obligations to similarly identified students highlights the need for better staff education.

### Chapter Sixteen: Sean, Traumatic Brain Injury

As the victim of documented brain injury, Sean's deviant sexual behavior was seen as a "compulsion" that had not diminished despite several consecutive prison terms. Between two such commitments, two children in his vicinity were murdered, and there was evidence of sexual molestation. The crime went unsolved for nine years until DNA advances revealed Sean as a match to this, and a second sex crime in Florida. After a hung jury in his first trial, the death penalty was imposed. This chapter concludes with a discussion of the state's current moratorium on capital punishment and the nationwide movement to abolish it altogether.

## Chapter Seventeen: Cory, Incompetent and Incapable

Although Cory was chronologically thirteen years old, he suffered with a rare genetic syndrome that reduced his mental age to the same level as his five-year-old victim. The touching incident occurred when he was inadvertently left alone with the little girl next door. Indeed, Cory's perseveration with body parts and lack of proper sex education should have raised bright red flags, but did not. Court advocacy resulted in personal counseling and reeducation intended to minimize the chance of recidivism.

## Chapter Eighteen: Young and Mentally Young Offenders

This chapter presents several individual cases where defendants as young as age seven entered the justice system. These include Jay, whose little feet dangled from his courtroom chair, intellectually disabled Donald, bullied at probation camp, and seventeen-year-old Jose, his red "juvy unit" jumpsuit flashing like a neon sign inside a men's jail facility. It also reviews statistics on trends in prosecuting and incarcerating juveniles, many with adult offenders. Finally, it poses the question, "At what age do we as a nation label a child as irredeemable?"

## Chapter Nineteen: Punishing Disabilities

This book would not be complete without a discussion of how disabled inmates fare once sentenced to prison. Having served as a principle expert in several class action lawsuits challenging unfair prison and parole practices for disabled inmates, I am aware that the outlook is grim. This chapter provides an in-depth discussion of problems unique to the disabled prison population due to their intellectual, attention, language, academic, and/or sensory-motor deficits. Accordingly, these inmates suffer greater hardships during incarceration than do their nondisabled peers.

## Chapter Twenty: My Video-less Lesson Plan

If I could have produced a video to deter high school students from stupid blunders that could lead to criminal activity, I would have chosen three charismatic young men as my "stars": twenty-year-old Tom, seventeen-year-old Mike, and eighteen-year-old Jason. All three had promising futures, but their dreams and plans were dashed on the fateful nights when outings with peers spiraled out of control. This chapter presents their stories, plus seven additional vignettes paired with discussion questions for teachers and parents to share with teenagers.

## Concluding Remarks: "Out Like Michael Jordan"

This final section issues a plea to the professional community to pursue and insure fundamental fairness for defendants, inmates, parolees, and victims with disabilities. My own retirement, though inevitable, left a gaping vacancy in the profession for qualified expert witnesses with first-hand knowledge of the cognitive disorders described in this book. Hopefully, reading their stories will inspire others to take up the fight.

Made in United States
North Haven, CT
04 November 2026

21770481R00171